japanese politics

Alfred A. Knopf, New York

japanese politics

patron-client democracy

Second Edition

Nobutaka Ike
Stanford University

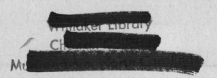

THIS IS A BORZOI BOOK PUBLISHED BY ALFRED A. KNOPF, INC.

Second Edition

First Printing

Library of Congress Cataloging in Publication Data

Ike, Nobutaka.
Japanese politics.

Bibliography: p.
1. Japan—Politics and government—1945-2.
Japan—Social conditions—1945-3. Japan—Economic conditions
—1945-I. Title.
JQ1618.I39 1972 320.9'52'04 75-38612
ISBN 0-394-31695-9

Manufactured in the United States of America

To Tai

preface

The first edition of *Japanese Politics* was written more than 15 years ago. Obviously, much has happened since then, with the result that the book is in some respects out-of-date. To begin with, the Japan of the mid-1950s was rather different from the Japan we know today. At that time, the country was in the process of recovery from the devastation and disruption caused by the war, and the new democratic government defined by the Constitution of 1946 was still of recent vintage.

Today as a result of phenomenal economic growth sustained throughout the 1960s, Japan is counted among the superpowers in terms of economic capability. Economic growth, moreover, has not only brought affluence to substantial sections of the population, but has also accelerated the trend toward increased urbanization and the shift in the working force from agriculture to industry. These and other kinds of social and economic changes have affected the nature of politics; but perhaps not to the extent that one might have anticipated. Japanese politics has been characterized by continuity, and by incremental rather than cataclysmic change. In this sense, the political situation in Japan differs sharply from that found in many countries in the so-called Third World where coups, rebellions, and revolutions occur from time to time. One of the consequences of this ability to change incrementally has been to give Japanese democracy an opportunity to mature and to become more firmly rooted with the passage of years.

The opportunity to reexamine the nature of Japanese democracy was one of the incentives that led me to respond affirmatively to the suggestion made by Mr. Barry Rossinoff, political science editor of the College Department of Alfred A. Knopf, that I write a revised edition of *Japanese Politics.* Furthermore, there appeared to be continuing interest in the earlier book that warranted a new edition, which would update the material, incorporate some of the findings of more recent scholarship on the Japanese economy, society, and polity, and, finally, bring to bear recent developments in empirical political theory on Japanese political data.

This second edition pretty much follows the general outline of the earlier work. The subtitle, however, has been changed in order to reflect the shift in emphasis that has occurred between the two editions. In the present one I have tried to articulate, although in a preliminary way, an outline of a democratic political system, which in essence has been imported from the West and grafted on to a social system that stresses the group rather than the individual.

I have argued that the product of such a combination represents yet another type of democracy—patron-client democracy—which is somewhat different from the Western models more familiar to us. If this approach is valid, it would then follow that Japanese democracy ought to be judged on its own terms rather than against norms and standards derived from Western experience. Also, I would like to suggest that the patron-client model of democracy might well prove to be more applicable to Asian democratic systems found in countries like India and the Philippines than the Western models.

Like every author, I am indebted to many people who have helped in one way or another. In particular I wish to acknowledge my indebtedness to my students, both graduate and undergraduate, who in my courses and seminars have asked penetrating questions and also made insightful comments on many phases of contemporary Japanese politics. I also wish to thank Miss Akiko Inui, who generously typed much of the manuscript. Mrs. Emiko Moffitt and Mr. Allan Paul, of the Japanese Collection in the Hoover Institution at Stanford, assisted me in locating source materials; and Miss Leona Huberman and Miss Jeannine Ciliotta, of the College Department of Alfred A. Knopf did an outstanding job of editing the manuscript. My wife gave me much help and support. I should add the customary statement that I alone am responsible for any errors and shortcomings.

Stanford, California
January 1972

Nobutaka Ike

contents

japanese politics

1 Incorporative Modernization

An Asian visitor stood on a busy intersection in downtown Tokyo, and as he looked at the forest of neon signs, the thousands of cars that choked the streets, and the long electric trains roaring along the overhead tracks, he shook his head and remarked, "This is not Asia."

Although Japan is geographically a part of Asia, it is not typically Asian in terms of technology and science, industrial organization, and economic development. In these respects, Japan is more akin to the advanced nations of the West.

MODERNIZATION

The development of Japan into an industrialized country without peer in Asia has occurred in a relatively short span of time, and has necessarily involved changes in almost every facet of life, from beliefs about the nature of the universe to dietary preferences. Analysts of Japanese affairs sometimes find it convenient to group these changes under the general rubric of "modernization." Indeed, the literature on modernization—that of Japan as well as of many other non-Western countries—grows constantly. In broad terms, the concept of modernization is used to describe a process by which a society becomes increasingly complex and heterogeneous. A modern industrial society is necessarily complex; it is characterized by a division of labor along occupational, skill, and class lines, and by a structure of government capable of regulating and directing a multitude of human efforts toward common and collective goals that are constructive rather than destructive.

It goes without saying that modernization as change implies movement away from something old to something new. We often use the term "traditional" in contrast to "modern." A traditional society is said to be transformed over a period of time by the process of social change into a modern society. Admittedly, there are problems with this kind of an approach: For instance, contemporary American society will undoubtedly continue to change, but if it is already modern, as most people think it is, what will it change to—postmodern perhaps? Nevertheless, this notion of change from a traditional state of affairs to a modern one has its uses, especially when we attempt to study the rapidly changing countries of the non-Western world.

Another problem that arises when we juxtapose traditional and modern is that we sometimes fall into the error of thinking that what is modern displaces what is traditional. This, of course, sometimes happens; the automobile pretty much displaced the horse and buggy as an important mode of land transportation. But in many instances, something modern does not necessarily displace what has existed traditionally. In Japan, for example, women tend to wear what is currently fashionable in Paris or Rome, but they also wear the Japanese kimono, a mode of dress inherited from their ancestors. In this case, modernity and tradition exist side by side. It would appear that the coexistence of the old and the new is particularly marked in the case of the modernization of Japan, and for this reason we have called this chapter "Incorporative Modernization." In modernizing, the Japanese sometimes cast off elements of their inherited culture, but they have also managed to retain much of it and to blend it with the new.

THE HISTORICAL PATTERN OF JAPANESE MODERNIZATION

The rapidity and magnitude of social change in recent decades should not blind us to the roots of modernity that go back prior to the opening of Japan to large-scale Western influences in the

1850s. Even in the Tokugawa period (1603–1868), Japan possessed features that are usually associated with modernity. To begin with, a sense of nationhood was already firmly established. Unlike some of the newer nations today, the Japanese did not have to suffer the travail of nation-building, of defining what it meant to be a Japanese. Very early in their history the Japanese had evolved a distinctive culture and a way of life that bound people together in a very fundamental way. The sense of allegiance to the nation remains strong today and is an overarching bond that transcends the ideological partisanship and bickering that often characterize contemporary partisan politics.

A second aspect of early modernity is urbanization. Modern societies are typically urban. By the Tokugawa period, cities and towns dotted the country and Edo (the old name for present-day Tokyo) had a population at least equal in size to London. There had evolved, moreover, a merchant class in the cities with its own subculture and mores. Urbanization was probably also associated with yet another mark of modernity—namely, literacy. A modern nation tied together by a communications network could not exist unless large numbers of people could read and write. In this regard, the Japanese experience was remarkable, for as R. P. Dore has shown, by the time of the Meiji Restoration (1868), 40 to 50 percent of all boys had received some schooling outside their homes, which suggests that literacy must have been quite high.[1]

Finally, the foundations for a bureaucracy, a necessary ingredient in a modern state, were laid in the Tokugawa period. Some members of the *samurai* class came to be employed as officials in the 250-odd feudal principalities that made up the Tokugawa political system. It was through their work as bureaucrats that they bettered their social and economic status, for the Tokugawa hegemony had eliminated the need for military prowess.

Thus, the foundations for large-scale modernization had already been laid when the country was opened up to Western

[1] R. P. Dore, "The Legacy of Tokugawa Education," in Marius B. Jansen (ed.), *Changing Japanese Attitudes Toward Modernization* (Princeton, N.J.: Princeton University Press, 1965), pp. 100–101.

influences in the middle of the nineteenth century. The story of Japan's transformation in the Meiji period (1868–1912) is fairly well known and need not be repeated here in detail. The point that ought to be stressed is that the samurai elite which came to power responded strongly to the external stimulus. They made the adverse comparison between the state of their nation and that of the great Western powers. As a result, they were determined to catch up with the West in order to achieve equality with the great powers. What followed was a program of purposive modernization directed mostly from above by a political elite drawn mainly from the old samurai class, and later by a bureaucracy chosen on the basis of achievement. Indeed, it appears that we have here an example of a modernizing bureaucracy that antedates by many decades the current attempts in many of the developing areas to modernize under government leadership.

One of the consequences of this pattern of modernization was the preservation, and even the strengthening, of many aspects of Japanese tradition. In particular, values, institutions, and practices having to do with social cohesion were purposely retained. For example, the closely knit family with the father as its authority figure was held up as the ideal. Moreover, the myth of the Japanese state structured as one large family descended from a common ancestor and owing loyalty to the patriarchical leader, the emperor, was deliberately fostered through the schools, the military establishment, the legal system, and official propaganda. In modernizing, the Japanese relied heavily on the West for technology and science, even for some social and political institutions; but when it came to those aspects of culture that affected the social cement, which enabled people to work together for national purposes, they rejected ideas like individualism, which appeared to be a divisive force. We ought to add a qualification, however. Although the culturally conservative position has been dominant, there has also been a minority "liberal" position whose proponents have argued for a rather thoroughgoing acceptance of Western institutions. This liberal position tends to be associated even today with higher education, and has led to tension between the Establishment and its critics, the intellectuals.

JAPANESE INDUSTRIALIZATION

Implicit in the goal of catching up with the West was a commitment to industrialization. Clearly, the way to national power and riches lay in industrial development, as the experience of the great powers had shown. The state therefore assumed an active role in economic development—a role it continues to play today. The government involved itself directly in some forms of enterprise (for instance, railroads), but for the most part it encouraged private entrepreneurs by a variety of methods—setting up model factories, sending students abroad for training, hiring foreign advisers, giving subsidies to business, and so on. One consequence of active government involvement in economic enterprise was the emergence of a few huge industrial combines, the *zaibatsu*, which came to dominate the economy until they were broken up to some extent by the trust-busting activities of the American Occupation after World War II. The prewar type of zaibatsu is gone, but there are still a small number of large firms commanding huge amounts of capital, using the most modern equipment, employing tens of thousands of workers, and competing on the world market with the leading Western companies. Some are almost household words in the West—Mitsubishi, Toyota, Hitachi, Toshiba, to mention a few.

Since such firms are visible, foreigners tend to assume that they typify the Japanese economy. The truth is that firms like Toyota sit atop a huge pyramid, the base of which is made up of a myriad of small firms, many of them tied to the big corporations, through a complex system of subcontracting. These small firms are more typical of a precapitalist economic order in the sense that they are generally family-owned enterprises with little capitalization and employing only a few workers. An example of the subcontracting system would be a situation in which an automobile manufacturer would have a series of parts suppliers, some of whom it helped set up by giving loans, providing obsolete machinery at low cost, and agreeing to purchase the output. If this subcontractor should prosper and expand his operations, he might then set up his own subcontractors, with the result that there would eventually exist tiers of such subcontractors. The bottom tier might well consist of small backalley workshops run by the family and one or two employees. Needless to say, labor efficiency and wage scales decline the further one drops down these series of tiers. This kind of economic structure is sometimes called a "dual economy," and it is not unique to Japan; there are counterparts in Italy and Spain. We can get an idea of the extent of the dual economy by comparing Japan with some Western countries. In 1966 a little over one-half of Japanese workers were employed in smaller plants, that is those employing between 1 and 99 persons, while the figure for the United Kingdom (1958) was one out of five. France with 40.6 percent was nearer the Japanese figure, while the United States with 26.2 percent and West Germany with 20.9 percent were closer to Britain.[2]

The notion of economic dualism could also be applied to the relationship between industry and agriculture. Just as economic development in Japan worked in such a way as to preserve to an astonishing degree premodern small-scale industry, so it has fostered the survival of small-scale agriculture. It is sometimes said that in industrialization a critical threshold is reached when the proportion of the total labor force engaged in agriculture falls below 50 percent. In the case of Japan, this level was reached in the mid-1920s, but as late as 1955 almost 40 percent were still in farming. Again it is instructive to compare this with England, where by 1950 only 5 percent of the labor force was engaged in farming. One reason for the survival of small-scale farming is to be found in state policy toward agriculture. Before the war, small farms were valued partly because the armed forces for national security reasons wanted the country to be as self-sufficient as possible in foodstuffs. Since the end of the war, national security considerations carry much less weight, but small-scale farmers have survived because they have been able to obtain economic benefits by exercising political leverage through the ruling Liberal Democratic party. Nevertheless, as we shall see later, urban industries have been draining manpower away from the rural areas.

[2] Tsuneta Yano Memorial Society, *Nippon; A Charter Survey*, 1969 edition, p. 167.

Our interest in economic dualism, of course, lies mostly in its political consequences. Despite industrialization, Japan still has a remarkably large number of individual entrepreneurs engaging in a variety of enterprises—farms, retail stores, repair shops, small workshops. There are, in addition, literally millions of family workers who help man these small enterprises. The magnitude of this category of persons can be seen in Table 1.

Table 1: Self-employed and Family Workers, 1965

	Number	Percentage
Employers and others working on own account	9,300,000	19.2%
Family workers	9,200,000	19.0
Total work force	48,300,000	100.0

Source: International Labour Office, *Year Book of Labour Statistics,* 1968 ed.

Almost 4 out of every 10 persons in the labor force either were self-employed in farming, industry, commerce, or service trades, or were working in enterprises owned by their families. As we will see later, the conservatives draw their support mainly from this group.

THE PROBLEM OF INDIVIDUALISM

There is no question that over the long run, modernization has increased what some people call "individuation." In an agrarian society, the individual is overshadowed by his family. The family head represents his family in the village assembly, and population is counted not in terms of the number of persons, but on the basis of the number of families present in the village. By contrast, in an industrialized capitalistic economy, the employer hires an individual who has the requisite skills, not the entire family. As individuation develops, a person begins to want things for himself, and relies on his own efforts to get them. He selects his beliefs and modes of behavior on the basis of principles of right and wrong that he has internalized, and he feels responsible for his own actions. David Riesman has argued that the "inner-directed man," a label which seems to fit what we have been describing, is the product of the post-Renaissance and Reformation Western society. He believes it to be associated with increased personal mobility, rapid capital accumulation, and expansion. In Western history, individuation came to be supported by an explicit creed, individualism, which justified the paramountcy of the individual.

In Japan, individualism as a creed has never taken root, perhaps because the country never passed through a period of laissez-faire economics. Actually, individualism has had a negative connotation in Japan; it has connoted such undesirable traits as nihilism, selfish egotism, and antisocial behavior. Even today, most Japanese do not wish to be individualists. Rather, they prefer to be a member of one group or another, even though group membership usually implies some suppression of individual desires and wishes in favor of group norms and goals. Of these groups, the family comprising the household group is important, but kinship outside the immediate household is not stressed, a fact that probably makes the Japanese family structure somewhat different from the extended family systems found in many other Asian countries.

Beyond the family are other groups based not on kinship relationships, but on a "personalized relation to a corporate group based on work, in which the major aspects of social and economic life are involved."[3] Chie Nakane, in a brilliant book on Japanese society, argues that this corporate group has a small functioning core of about one to two dozen members, hierarchically arranged according to the seniority principle, and bound together by strong emotional ties. The individuals of superior and inferior status form *oyabun-kobun* or patron-client relationships. She adds, moreover, that "the overall picture of society resulting from such inter-personal (and inter-group) relations is not that of horizontal stratification by class or caste but of vertical stratification by institution or group of institutions."[4] Japanese society, therefore, is one in which vertical rather than horizontal ties predominate.

[3] Chie Nakane, *Japanese Society* (Berkeley, Calif.: University of California Press, 1970), p. 7.
[4] *Ibid.*, p. 87.

It should be noted, by way of qualification, that the spread of democratic norms has had some effect on interpersonal relationships; there has been a shift toward more horizontal ties with peers based on more egalitarian views. That this should occur is perhaps to be expected, given the tempo of modernization in recent years. But the point that ought to be stressed here is that while many changes have occurred at the macro level through such agencies as the mass media and the educational system, comparable changes have not occurred at the micro level. Japan is still a country where, as David Plath has put it, the self is underdeveloped in an overdeveloped social order.[5]

In the West, the rise of political democracy went hand in hand with the growth of individualism. It is tempting to believe that the Western pattern will be repeated as the process of modernization spreads around the world. There are both foreigners and Japanese who argue that Japan should follow in the footsteps of the more advanced Western countries and experience a period of liberalism and individualism, but it may well be that reality will prove to be otherwise. There is no compelling reason to believe that democracy in Asia and Africa will necessarily possess the same features that characterize democratic systems in the West. As we shall see in the chapters that follow, contemporary Japan is a democracy, but it is not exactly the same kind of democracy as Great Britain and the United States.

[5] David W. Plath, *The After Hours* (Berkeley, Calif.: University of California Press, 1964), p. 177.

2 Japanese Political Culture and Democracy

Most of the time, politics involves collective action on the part of numerous individuals. What makes such collective action possible is political culture, which Sidney Verba has defined as "the system of empirical beliefs, expressive symbols and values which defines the situation in which political action takes place."[1] Stated in another way, political culture has to do with psychological variables, that is, with the attitudes and orientations of individuals toward politics. These attitudes and orientations are widely shared because they are learned through transmission from one generation to another, through the family, schools, the mass media—in short, through the socialization process. Since these attitudes are shared, individuals, when stimulated by political symbols, personalities or events, are led to participate in joint or reciprocal action.

One would expect that in stable societies the political culture would change rather slowly. By contrast, in revolutionary situations, there are likely to be drastic transformations in political culture that will often be purposefully induced by the ruling elite. In the case of Japan we do not have, of course, a revolutionary situation, but still there has been a certain amount of discontinuity occasioned by the innovations, particularly in the institutional structure (see Chapter 3), imposed by the Occupation forces after 1945. The main thrust of Occupation policy was to encourage more individualistic beliefs and be-

[1] Sidney Verba, "Comparative Political Culture," in Lucian W. Pye and Sidney Verba (eds.), *Political Culture and Political Development* (Princeton, N.J.: Princeton University Press, 1969), p. 513.

havior. While it cannot be denied that the Occupation did leave its mark and that more recent social change has also helped to modify Japanese political culture, the surprising thing is that the magnitude of change has remained remarkably small. As we have suggested in the previous chapter, in political culture as in many other areas, modernity has not swept away tradition.

TRADITION VS. MODERNITY

What do we mean by tradition and by modernity in political culture? In the present context, tradition refers to social values that have been handed down from the past. Specifically, it is the expectation that the individual will be subordinated to the group, whether it be the family, village, work gang, business firm, or club. Subordination implies that an individual's norms will be congruent with those of the group, that he will work for the good of his group, and that he will be loyal to it. By contrast, modernity suggests a more autonomous person. This does not mean that he is antisocial, but rather that he thinks for himself, that he makes "rational" choices among alternative courses of social action, that he is not compulsively submissive to political authority.

Some empirical data on Japanese attitudes related to tradition and modernity are available. One important source is the nationwide survey on national character carried out by the Institute of Mathematical Statistics in Tokyo at five-year intervals beginning in 1953. These surveys contained a battery of questions designed to get at the problem of tradition versus modernity. The findings indicate that over the years there has been a gradual but nevertheless persistent shift in attitudes in the direction of modernity. But although there were a number of questions that elicited agreement from the majority of respondents, relatively few individuals (a little more than 10 percent) agreed consistently with all these questions. That is, on some questions individuals belonged with the majority, but on others they did not. Stated another way, there were certain attitudes that may be considered to be typically Japanese, but there were only a small percentage of typically Japanese individuals. This suggests the likelihood that relatively few individuals are consistently traditional or modern in their attitudes; rather, each person represents a varying mixture of traditional and modern views.

It is, however, possible to generalize as to who is likely to be more modern. Education appears to exert a powerful influence. That this should be so is not altogether surprising; education usually makes people more skeptical, critical, and independent. Educated people are less likely to submit themselves to the pull of social conformity. But even education has not succeeded in removing the traditional penchant for paternalism and the dependency it implies. One of the questions asked in the survey had to do with attitudes toward one's work supervisor.

> Let us assume that there are two types of section chiefs; if you were to work under one of them, which one [of the following] would you prefer?
>
> 1. He does not make unreasonable demands that violate work rules, but he does not look after you in matters that do not pertain to your work.
> 2. Sometimes he makes unreasonable demands that violate work rules, but he looks after you even in matters that have nothing to do with your work.

More than 70 percent of those questioned preferred the supervisor who, although a hard taskmaster, was willing to look after one's personal and other non-work-related needs. Moreover, response to this question has varied little over the fifteen-year span covered by the surveys. Equally interesting, the response is remarkably uniform, whether the person giving the answer is young or old, uneducated or educated, worker or professional. In short, age, education, and occupation, which are important variables when it comes to other questions, appear to have little effect.

Table 2 shows the results of another study that probed attitudes of both American and Japanese industrial workers. The question was: "When a worker wishes to marry, I think his (her) superior should ______."

Table 2

Reply	U.S.	Japan
1. Help select a possible mate and serve as a go-between	2%	6%
2. Offer personal advice to the worker if requested	29	70
3. Merely present a small gift from the company	9	19
4. Not be involved in such a personal matter	60	5

Source: Arthur Whitehill, Jr., and Shin-ichi Takezawa, *The Other Worker* (Honolulu: East-West Center Press, 1968), p. 171. Reprinted by permission of the publisher.

As can be seen, the majority of American workers in the sample did not wish their supervisors to be involved in their personal lives, whereas the majority of Japanese workers did. The evidence again suggests that many Japanese prefer paternalistic, diffuse, all-embracing relationships—in other words, patron-client relationships.

ATTITUDES TOWARD AUTHORITY

What effect, if any, does preference for paternalism have on attitudes toward politics? Here it is not possible to give a simple, clear-cut answer. A logical extension of patron-client relationships into the larger political setting would be rule by a strong man, a kind of benevolent dictator. But it is evident that the Japanese have avoided rule by a strong man and have preferred to operate through groups. The national character surveys cited above have tried to measure sentiment toward one-man rule. They have asked this question: "There is this view: Let us say we want to make Japan a better country, and if an outstanding political leader appeared, it would be better to leave everything up to him rather than for the people to debate among themselves." The percentage of those approving this statement has declined from 43 percent in 1953 to 30 percent in

1968, while the number of those disapproving it has risen from 38 percent in 1953 to 51 percent in 1968.[2]

There would appear to be a fundamental consensus that the government in power must periodically appeal to the electorate for confirmation of its privilege to continue in office. There are numerous examples of countries in the so-called Third World in which the leader will declare that he intends to keep his office for life, or in which tanks roll in the streets to signal a change in government. This sort of thing has not occurred in Japan since 1945, and it is hard to imagine it happening—an observation that seems to attest to the existence of a consensus in favor of democratic rules of the game. Moreover, the longer that these rules are followed, the more firmly established they will become. Democracy, like good whiskey, improves with age.

Yet it is curious that despite this commitment to democracy, those who manage to get into office via the democratic method enjoy so little public esteem. Robert Ward has noted that "politics and politicians in the abstract are not usually regarded as being particularly trustworthy."[3] This negative view also extends to political parties, which consist for the most part of an organized group of politicians. One interpretation of this phenomenon advanced by a Japanese political scientist, Jun-ichi Kyogoku, is that the Japanese people believe government authority should be fair and impartial; when they see politicians behaving in a partisan manner and sometimes involved in corrupt practices, they feel great disappointment and moral indignation.[4] So far, this lack of trust in politicians has not become severe enough to seriously undermine support for the democratic system.

Another phenomenon related to aversion to partisanship is an unwillingness to accept the notion of majority rule. A basic premise of Western democratic thought is that when unanimity does not exist, decisions should be in accordance with the wishes of the majority. There is a further understanding that the

[2] Tokeisuri Kenkyujo, *Kokumin-sei no Kenkyu* [Study of National Character] (Tokyo, 1968), p. 126.

[3] Robert E. Ward, "Japan: The Continuity of Modernization," in Pye and Verba, *op. cit.*, p. 71.

[4] Jun-ichi Kyogoku, "Changes in Political Image and Behavior," *Journal of Social and Political Ideas in Japan*, II, 3 (December 1964), 122.

rights of the minority are to be respected and that the minority has the privilege of trying in the future to become a majority. Institutional devices are sometimes provided to protect a minority from the majority; for example, the filibuster in the American Congress. Still, as a practical method of getting work done, the idea of majority rule is widely followed. In Japan (and this is also true in many other parts of Asia), the time-honored method of arriving at decisions is through consensus. This method rests on the premise that members of a group—say, a village council—should continue to talk, bargain, make concessions, and so on until finally a consensus emerges. The result is that the group remains unified, and does not split into a majority and a minority. Despite the spread of democratic norms, this tradition of rule by consensus still has its appeal and sometimes leads to cries against the "tyranny of the majority"—for example, when the ruling party with its majority pushes through legislation over the strong protests of the opposition.

So far we have been concerned with who should govern and in what manner; now we turn to the issue of what the government should do. One of the important purposes of government is to solve problems that arise through collective action. A striking characteristic of twentieth-century developments in many parts of the world is the increasing tendency to turn to government when difficulties arise, for the increasing differentiation and complexity in modern societies make it difficult—if not impossible—for individuals to find solutions. Some obvious current examples are pollution of the environment and the decay of large cities. The frequency with which governments are implored to help solve problems, however, varies from country to country, and appears to be related to the political culture—that is, to the attitudes people have about what government ought and ought not to do. As David Easton has written: "The cultural norms, transmitted across the generations, dictate and regulate which wants a member is expected to solve for himself or in cooperation with others, and which it is acceptable in the society for the members to seek to fulfill through political action."[5] To take one example, in modern socie-

[5] David Easton, *A Systems Analysis of Political Life* (New York: Wiley, 1965), p. 103.

ties the problem of social welfare for the individual buffeted by economic adversity, illness, or old age demands attention; yet a Japanese commentator is critical of the Western European view that the state should be responsible. So far as he is concerned, in Japan there are three instruments for coping with such problems: the family, life insurance companies, and the employer. Only those individuals who do not have access to these instruments should rely on the state.[6]

It would appear then that in many instances cultural norms inhibit people from seeking to satisfy their wants and needs through organized political action. One practical consequence of such inhibitions is that the danger of countless demands overloading the political systems is very much lessened. The burden of political leadership is made that much lighter, and the possibilities of continued stability are enhanced.

A MODEL OF PATRON-CLIENT DEMOCRACY

The preceding comments on Japanese political culture, brief as they are, have already suggested that Japanese democracy is somewhat different from the Western systems with which we are more familiar. In order to better understand this type of democracy, let us compare it with different "models" of democratic systems.

1. The Rational Choice Model. The expectation here is that all citizens are both well informed about political issues and problems and highly interested. Moreover, these citizens, on the basis of their information and interest, participate regularly and actively in politics. They not only vote, but also discuss politics with their friends and neighbors, join political organizations, and make their wishes known to their legislative representatives. In addition, they have a clear understanding of the feasible alternative courses of political action, and are capable of choosing one of these on the basis of enlightened self-inter-

[6] Jiro Sakamoto, "Nihon-teki Fukushi Kokka no Koso" [Conception of a Japanese-style Welfare State], *Chuo Koron,* 79, 12 (December 1964), 70.

est. Clearly, this is an idealized picture of democracy, one that is rarely achieved in practice.

2. The Civic Culture Model. This is a more elitist model of democracy. It presupposes that the body of citizens would contain various kinds of individuals, ranging from those who are apathetic to those who are active in political affairs. Political participation, however, will be intermittent rather than continuous and will ordinarily be mediated by voluntary associations of one kind or another. Most of the time, citizens will be willing to leave the job of government to the political elite. They feel confident that if the need arises, they will be able to interpose themselves into the political system and thus influence political outcomes. The British political system can be taken as a typical example of this kind of model.

3. The Pluralistic Democracy Model. This model postulates the existence of not one but a number of power centers. Power will therefore be dispersed, and for that reason, limited. Even the ability of the majority to have its way will be circumscribed by the veto power of the minority or minorities. The effect is to limit coercion and to encourage constant negotiation among the power centers, thus enhancing the ability to maximize consent and the resolution of conflict through peaceful means. Perhaps the most conspicuous example of this model would be the American political system.

The model suggested for Japan is different from all of these, yet combines elements from each.

4. The Patron-Client Model. Like the civic culture model, this is essentially an elitist type. Given the predominance of vertical relationships between patrons and clients, voluntary associations, which depend on horizontal ties, are developed in only a rudimentary way. Individuals therefore tend to relate to the political system through their patrons, who typically are local notables, political bosses, union leaders, local politicians, and leaders of local organizations. Those who are not involved in patron-client relationships are likely to be apathetic; if they participate in politics at all, they do so haphazardly and intermittently.

In this model, voters tend to trade their ballots for anticipated benefits that are particularistic in character—that is, for jobs and favors for themselves or their relatives; schools, roads, hospitals, and other public works projects for the community. Political issues and questions of ideology are relatively unimportant. Under these circumstances, inputs in the form of demands for broadly conceived public policy are negligible.

This type of democracy will work reasonably well provided two conditions are met: (1) There exists some source within the political system that originates inputs calling for public policy outputs. (2) The demands for particularistic pork-barrel projects do not escalate to the extent that they overload the capacity of the system to meet them. In the case of Japan, the two conditions appear to be met, but we will defer further discussion of this point to Chapters 7 and 11.

3 The Political Structure

The formal structure of any government is seldom fully congruent with the realities of political power, but it can often provide clues to the prevailing state of political affairs. Democratic government rests on a set of "rules of the game" that define the allocation of formal authority among the branches of government, the rules of policy making and execution, the definition of what constitutes the legitimate acts of government, and the ends implicit in the constitutional structure. Knowledge of these rules is therefore helpful in understanding how the political system works.

THE CONSTITUTION

Normally, a constitution results from the interplay of historical, legal, and political forces, and seeks to give expression to shared ideals and values. The present Japanese Constitution, enacted as an amendment to the 1889 Meiji Constitution in late 1946, does not fit this pattern because it was written—rather hurriedly—by the American Occupation authorities and in effect imposed on the Japanese government, which after a desultory debate in the parliament, accepted it as the basic law of the land. It is not surprising, given its origins, that the Constitution should stress liberal democratic values and goals. If the Japanese had been given a free hand in writing their constitution, they would undoubtedly have stressed traditional Japanese values, and produced a more authoritarian and paternalistic document.

The Constitution provides for the first time a single, all-embracing, organic law for the country. Unlike the Meiji Constitution which it replaced, the present Constitution proclaims in its preamble the doctrine of popular sovereignty. "We, the Japanese people, acting through our duly elected representatives in the National Diet, . . . do proclaim that sovereign power resides with the people and do firmly establish this Constitution."

There follow 11 chapters of varying length. Chapter I defines the position of the emperor (see below). Chapter II contains the controversial Article 9, in which ". . . the Japanese people forever renounce war as a sovereign right of the nation and the threat or use of force as a means of settling international disputes," and which also affirms that ". . . land, sea, and air forces, as well as other war potential, will never be maintained." Chapter III, the "Rights and Duties of the People," guarantees a long list of popular rights and is intended to provide a full measure of civil liberties. Chapters IV and V relate to the structure and power of the National Diet and the Cabinet. Chapter VI regulates the judiciary, while Chapter VII deals with finance. Local self-government is taken up in Chapter VIII. Chapter IX provides for amendments which ". . . shall be initiated by the Diet, through a concurring vote of two-thirds or more of all the members of each House and shall thereupon be submitted to the people for ratification, which shall require the affirmative vote of a majority of all votes cast thereon, at a special referendum or at such election as the Diet shall specify." Chapter X enunciates the principle that the Constitution shall be the supreme law of the land; and Chapter XI contains supplementary provisions, mostly having to do with the transition from the old to the new Constitution.

The Constitution clearly provides the legal framework for a democratic system of government; but the real test, of course, is whether the legal formula can be translated into political reality. The authors of an official publication issued by the Occupation in 1949 admitted that "the new Constitution is as yet no more than a new set of rules, devised in committee and communicated to the players, in [sic] which the players have as yet little familiarity or confidence. It will take time and experience before they know the rules well enough to play by them."[1]

It is little wonder, then, that the more traditionally oriented political leaders should express unhappiness over a Constitution which they regard as an alien document. Ironically, its chief defenders are the Socialists, who consistently oppose American foreign policy as being imperialistic. As for the public, the Constitution so far has not evoked warm emotional response. In one survey, only about 1 out of 4 of those interviewed said they liked the Constitution. One would suppose that almost everyone would have views about the no-war clause which, because of its controversial nature, has been widely discussed in the press. Yet about a third of the people who are asked about it in public opinion surveys consistently refuse to take a stand and give a "don't know" response. The Constitution has so far not been amended because the opposition parties who wish to retain it have managed to win at least one-third of the seats in the legislature, enough to prevent changes (amendments require a two-thirds vote plus a favorable referendum).

THE EMPEROR

Under the Constitution, the emperor, who was previously considered divine and the source of all legal authority and political power, is ". . . the symbol of the State and of the unity of the people, deriving his position from the will of the people with whom resides sovereign power." The emperor is to perform ". . . only such acts in matters of state as are provided for in this Constitution and he shall not have powers related to government." Like many monarchs, the emperor promulgates laws and treaties, convokes the Diet, attests the appointment and dismissal of ministers of state and other high officials, receives foreign ambassadors and ministers, and performs ceremonial functions; but he performs these acts with "the advice and

[1] Supreme Commander for the Allied Powers, *Political Reorientation of Japan* (Washington, D.C.: Government Printing Office, 1949), Vol. 1, p. 117.

approval of the Cabinet," and "on behalf of the people." The emperor quite clearly reigns, but does not rule.

Conservative politicians have on occasion urged that the Constitution be amended so that the emperor could become the "head of the state." They apparently feel that the affective side of politics is also important. In Britain the royal family helps to enrich the ceremonial aspect of political life; and there is something to be said, particularly in a culture like the Japanese where personalized relationships are important, for using living symbols, rather than abstract ones like the Constitution, to generate feelings of loyalty to the political community. But because of left-wing opposition, a constitutional amendment along these lines is not feasible, and in any case, it would appear from the results of public opinion surveys that most people prefer the present arrangement.

Although among many young people the emperor has a rather negative image and some have been known to make derogatory remarks about him, it is difficult to judge the extent and depth of such feelings. The marriage of the Crown Prince to Michiko Shoda, daughter of the owner of Japan's largest flour mill, certainly elicited a great deal of popular enthusiasm. Yet in an era when kings have been toppled in many places, one sometimes wonders if the emperor system will survive in the long run. There is also the question of whether the imperial house today possesses residual power that could be exercised in case of a grave national emergency. In 1945, when Japan was confronted by the most serious crisis of the twentieth century, it was the emperor who tipped the scales in favor of peace. Whether the throne could act in a similar manner in another emergency is very problematical.

THE CABINET

Almost everywhere, the executive exercises tremendous influence over the government, and this is also true in Japan. Without cabinet leadership, policy making would be greatly hampered.

The Japanese cabinet is composed of the prime minister, who in turn appoints (and removes) his ministers of state. The

Constitution requires only that the majority of ministers be members of the Diet, but very few non-Diet members have been named to cabinet posts.

The prime minister, who is quite clearly the most visible figure in the government, is in theory elected by the National Diet, but that election is a formality so long as one party holds a majority and can come to an agreement on who its leader should be. In effect, the prime minister is chosen by the Liberal Democratic party convention that elects the party president. This election can be a complicated affair, because the party is in essence a federation of factions, and any faction leader, if he is to win the majority of votes in the convention, must build a coalition of factions by promising tangible rewards, such as cabinet posts, to those willing to ally with him. Leiserson has argued that a good deal of what goes on in the election of the party president can be explained by the use of game theory.[2]

One indicator of political stability is the durability of cabinets. Japan has been spared the spectacle of the frequent fall of cabinets, the frantic efforts of prime ministers to put together a viable coalition, and prolonged periods of caretaker governments. Since 1955, when the Liberal Democratic party was formed through the merger of two smaller conservative parties, there have been five prime ministers to date (1971): Hatoyama, Ishibashi, Kishi, Ikeda, and Sato. And three of these had to leave office because of illness.

Although prime ministers tend to stay on, their colleagues come and go. Every prime minister reshuffles his cabinet almost annually. He brings in a certain number of new people in order to reward them for past support and to ensure support in the future when he comes up for reelection as party president. (The president is elected for a two-year term.) The prime minister's control over cabinet membership gives him a good deal of political capital, since every politician wants a cabinet post, even if for only a short time, because of the prestige this gives him. Moreover, cabinet status usually enhances one's ability to get votes in the next election. The frequent reshuffling of

[2] Michael Leiserson, "Factions and Coalitions in One-party Japan: An Interpretation Based on the Theory of Games," *American Political Science Review*, 62, 3 (September 1968), 770–87.

the cabinet is therefore understandable, but its effect on the operation of the ministries may not be altogether salutary. Few ministers have their jobs long enough to learn very much about how a particular ministry works.

One notable difference between Japanese cabinet members and their counterparts in other democratic countries is personality makeup. One looks in vain for the Japanese equivalent of Franklin Delano Roosevelt, Winston Churchill, or Pandit Nehru. Japanese political leaders are colorless and singularly lacking in charisma. No doubt Japanese society produces colorful individuals, but the mechanism that recruits leaders seems to screen out such persons. Qualities such as a magnetic personality and oratorical skill are unimportant. What counts are those things that make one a good patron—namely, the ability to raise money, taking a personal interest in one's followers, loyalty to the group, personal connections with other leaders, and skill in bargaining and making behind-the-scenes deals.

These comments would certainly apply to recent Japanese prime ministers and the cabinet members. Except for Hatoyama, who came up via Tokyo city politics and had a certain amount of flair, prime ministers since 1955 have been mostly bureaucratic types. Eisaku Sato was a career civil servant in the National Railways before his subsequent rise to leadership of the Liberal Democratic party. His predecessor, Hayato Ikeda, was also a civil servant who had spent most of his time in the Ministry of Finance dealing with tax matters. As for the cabinet members, they are for the most part older men; only a few have been under fifty years of age. Moreover, they tend to be highly educated. The majority have been college graduates, with a disproportionately large number coming from the prestigious government universities. They differ from the British cabinet in that they are not drawn from the upper social class—meritocracy rather than aristocracy is the norm in Japanese politics.

THE NATIONAL DIET

Before World War II, the national legislature was known as the Imperial Diet; today it is called the National Diet. Japan was the first Asian country to establish a popularly elected legislature (1890). To be sure, most of the time the Imperial Diet played only a minor role because the cabinet and other executive agencies could pretty much ignore it if they so desired. Its most important function was to act as a sounding board for public opinion. The American framers of the 1946 Constitution sought to elevate the National Diet in prestige and in power. For the first time, legislators were provided with amenities and services to aid them in their work: they were given private offices and franking privileges, and a National Diet Library and a legislative reference service were established. The Constitution states that "The Diet shall be the highest organ of state power, and shall be the sole law-making organ of the State."

It would be a mistake, of course, to assume that the National Diet is what the Constitution says it is. That it participates in the legislative process is not to be denied; but as is true in the case of the British Parliament, it is difficult to be much more precise than that. One thing is clear: Not much legislation originates in the Diet; rather, most of it comes from the government agencies via the cabinet. This does not mean, however, that the government can push through any piece of legislation it wants. The National Diet can and does exercise a kind of veto power, especially because of the presence of opposition parties. In subsequent chapters we will consider in detail the various roles of the Diet in the governmental process; suffice it to say here that there is an interplay involving the government in power, the legislature, and the public.

Of the two houses that comprise the National Diet, the lower house, the House of Representatives, is the more important. It is a large body, consisting at present of 491 legislators chosen from 123 electoral districts plus Okinawa. The term of office is four years, but the house is often dissolved before the term is completed. When this happens, a new election must be held within 40 days.

The chamber of the House of Representatives is laid out in a semicircle, with the Speaker seated at the center in front. He is flanked on both sides by his assistants and by cabinet members. The majority party (the Liberal Democratic party) sits on the left-hand side (viewed from the back of the chamber), while the opposition parties are seated on the right. Unlike the British House of Commons, the first- and second-term members sit near the front; those with seniority sit at the back.

Every legislative body develops mores in the course of its historical development. In contrast to the British Parliament, politeness, decorum, and strict adherence to the rules of procedure do not appear to be characteristic of the House of Representatives. Sometimes opposition members will make so much noise with their catcalls and shouts that it will be virtually impossible to hear a prime minister's speech in the chamber. On rare occasions violence will break out; a favorite tactic is to try to prevent the Speaker from getting to his seat by blocking the passageway. The government sometimes rams legislation through by devious parliamentary maneuvers like locking out the opposition. Although it is hard to prove, it seems reasonable to assume that the behavior of legislators has not exactly endeared them to the public at large. During demonstrations in the vicinity of the Diet, participants have been known to urinate against the main doors of the Diet building to indicate their contempt for the institution.

The upper chamber, the House of Councillors, replaced the old House of Peers, which became an anomaly when the Occupation abolished the nobility. The House of Councillors is composed of 252 members who serve six-year terms. One-half of the upper chamber stands for election every three years. The selection of members is divided: 150 are elected from the prefectures (plus 2 from Okinawa); the remaining 100 are elected from the nation at large. Each voter casts two votes, one for a prefectural candidate and one for a national candidate. The intent in establishing the House of Councillors was that it would show "sound judgment" and be a stabilizing force should the lower house run to extremes. The belief was that those elected from the nation at large would be individuals who had distinguished themselves in their various professions and who would therefore lend the weight of their prestige to Diet deliberations. It was also anticipated that the upper house would be free of partisan politics.

Under the Constitution, bills must be passed by both houses. Any differences that might arise are ironed out in joint conference committees. The House of Representatives can override an adverse vote in the upper house by passing the bill again by a two-thirds majority. On certain matters—for example, the budget and treaties—concurrence by the House of Councillors is not necessary, provided that the lower house approves it at least one month prior to the end of the legislative session. The House of Representatives is quite clearly the more powerful body, but the House of Councillors does play a definite role in the legislative process.

Given this fact, it is not surprising that political parties were soon established in the House of Councillors. The government party, with a majority in the House of Representatives, was not about to sit idly by and see its legislative program stalled in the upper house. In addition, the notion that the national constituency would bring in distinguished individuals proved to be not particularly realistic. In order to be elected from the nation at large, a person had to have some organization, such as a religious group or a labor union, to mobilize the vote for him or be well known in his own right, like a television personality or a government official. Finally, the House of Councillors has not been completely free of disorderly proceedings, so that it has in many ways not always lived up to the ideal of a body that would exercise "sound judgment." Proposals for its reform—for example, having some of its members appointed rather than elected —have been put forward from time to time, but as yet nothing concrete has been done.

In most legislative bodies, much of the business is done in committees, and the National Diet is no exception. As part of the reforms sponsored by the Occupation, the standing committee system of the American Congress was adopted. There are standing committees for each major field of legislation: foreign affairs, budget, education, labor, agriculture, commerce, transportation, audit, disciplinary, and so on. In the House of Representatives, committee chairmanships go to members of the ruling Liberal Democratic party, but in the House of Councillors some chairmanships have been given to the opposition Socialist party. Chairmen, of course, are in a position to exercise a great deal of leverage. The most sought-after committees are those that provide opportunities for promoting pork-barrel projects; others, such as cabinet, foreign relations, finance, and steering, do not have many members eager to serve. It comes as no surprise that the appropriations committee should have many aspirants and hence be large: In the lower house, the committee has about fifty members; in the House of Councillors, there are about forty-five members.

Committees hold public meetings at which witnesses may testify. Cabinet members have to be prepared to spend many hours in committee meetings being questioned by the legislators, especially those in the opposition parties. Each ministry has officials known as "government members" who accompany cabinet ministers to these meetings in order to help them answer questions. Finally, the standing committees each have staff specialists and researchers. In each house there are 14 specialists and just under 100 researchers.

A criticism often voiced of the committee system is that special relationships have come to be established between the ministries and the corresponding committee in the Diet; for example, between the Ministry of Agriculture and the Agricultural Committee. The same kind of criticism is sometimes made of American government agencies that allegedly have been "captured" by the industries they are supposed to regulate. Everywhere, it would seem, politics seldom operates in an ideal way.

THE JUDICIARY

In the prewar period, the judiciary was under the control of the executive, especially the Ministry of Justice. Under the new Constitution, the judiciary was made independent and its power and prestige substantially raised. The idea of judicial review was introduced, presumably in order to make the high tribunal a watchdog of the Constitution. According to Article 81, "The Supreme Court is the court of last resort with power to determine the constitutionality of any law, order, regulation or official act." Today the courts form a separate organization headed by the Supreme Court. In keeping with the independent status of the judiciary, the Supreme Court supervises judicial administration. Provision is also made for funds to be independently appropriated in the national budget.

The Supreme Court is composed of the Chief Judge, who is appointed by the emperor upon designation by the cabinet, and fourteen associate judges, who are appointed directly by the cabinet. At least ten of the judges must have high professional qualifications in the legal field, but the remaining four may be outstanding persons in other fields. Supreme Court judges serve until they reach the retirement age of seventy. A popular check is provided by a system of recall elections in which the judges must be approved by the electorate every ten years, but in actuality this is mostly a formality. In order to prevent the Supreme Court from assuming too heavy a burden, its jurisdiction is limited to appeal cases requiring a review of issues of law. The provision for dissenting opinions is an innovation in Japanese court procedure, one that has been used in the postwar courts.

At present, below the Supreme Court there are eight high courts whose districts correspond to the eight geographical regions of Japan. The high courts take up appeals cases that do not fall within the jurisdiction of the Supreme Court. Below the high courts are district courts (at present 49, roughly one for each prefecture). The district court has original jurisdiction over serious crimes and civil suits involving large sums, and appellate jurisdiction over cases originating in the summary courts. There are more than 500 summary courts, and their jurisdiction is limited to minor criminal matters and civil suits involving small sums. There are also family courts, which use informal procedures in trying to settle domestic relations cases.

The role of the courts in the Japanese political process is influenced by the prevailing attitudes toward law and the court system. Most people prefer to settle disputes through a compromise arrangement arrived at with the mediation of friends, relatives, or influential persons, rather than engage in litigation in the courts. Japanese traditionally have preferred amicable and harmonious social relations, and such relations would be jeopardized by clear-cut court decisions based on the assertion of the legal rights of individuals. This attitude toward litigation is reflected in the small number of practicing lawyers in Japan.

There are about 8 lawyers per 100,000 persons, as opposed to 150 in the United States. It is also true, however, that some of the functions performed by American lawyers are handled in Japan by legal specialists and by graduates of law faculties in various universities who have knowledge of the law, but who have not been professionally trained as lawyers.

Given this background, it is not surprising that the courts have not aggressively sought to assert their influence. The Supreme Court, for example, has declared some administrative actions unconstitutional, but it has refrained from overturning major pieces of legislation. In 1959 the Court reviewed a case that sought to declare illegal the maintenance of American military bases in Japan on the ground that the Security Treaty with the United States violated the no-war clause in the Constitution. The court, however, upheld the treaty.

It is quite possible, of course, that in time social change will modify traditional attitudes. According to one recent book, "a sweeping change in the traditional attitude towards litigation has appeared. More and more people in Japan, especially in the business world, are becoming aware of the necessity for arriving at reasonable and enforceable solutions by means of the courts rather than at amicable but unenforceable settlements outside of the courts."[3]

LOCAL GOVERNMENT

Before the war, Japan was a centralized, unitary state. The central government exercised considerable control over local government through the now-defunct Ministry of Home Affairs, which appointed the prefectural governors. As part of its program to democratize Japan, the American Occupation sought to promote "grass roots democracy" by providing for a larger measure of local autonomy. Toward this end, the Local Autonomy Law of 1947 was enacted. It increased the number of elective offices—for example, prefectural governors and mayors

[3] Teisuke Akamatsu, "Legal Practices," in Robert Ballon (ed.), *Doing Business in Japan* (Tokyo: Sophia University–Tuttle, 1967), p. 137.

were now elected and in theory made responsible to prefectural assemblies and city councils, respectively. The system of recall and initiative was also instituted in order to give voters more control over local officials.

Despite the law, the actual amount of local autonomy that prevails is rather limited. The country is small—about the size of some of the larger American states—and the prefectures (of which there are 46) are more akin to counties than to states. Many activities are regulated by central government laws, and so local government entities in effect administer regulations emanating from Tokyo. There are even "model laws," which are drafted by the central government and which local governments dutifully pass. The predominant position of Tokyo is reflected in the dependence of local governments on subsidies and grants-in-aid from the central government to meet their financial needs, since they have not been given extensive taxing power. Every prefectural government maintains offices in Tokyo, and there is a steady stream of official delegations from local government entities at all levels coming to the capital to plead for more money.

There has been some talk among conservatives that the old system of appointed governors should be revived, a move that would no doubt be strongly resisted by opposition forces, since there are some Socialist-backed governors and mayors. One change that has been made, however, is the elimination of locally elected school boards, a system created by the Occupation, in favor of appointed school boards and more centralized control of education through the Ministry of Education.

In sum, in local government, as in the case of the judicial system, the intent of the Occupation-sponsored reforms has not been fulfilled. Local autonomy in the true sense does not exist because of the dependence of local governments on the central government. What about the relationship between the local government and the citizens? Here, some break with traditional patterns is becoming evident. The nature of local political leadership and popular participation appears to be changing.

In rural areas, the hamlet or *buraku* has long been the basic unit in local politics. The hamlet is characterized generally by a high degree of solidarity; its leaders are likely to be the local notables—wealthy landowners, merchants, long-time residents of the area; and decisions on public matters are arrived at through discussion and consensus rather than by means of voting and majority rule. Electoral participation, however, is high, especially for local elections. This is not because the residents show a high degree of political consciousness, but rather because a high turnout rate is considered a matter of pride for the hamlet. In short, the hamlet residents are mobilized in the name of hamlet solidarity.

This type of political style still prevails in the more isolated rural areas, but in recent years the tempo of urbanization has been stepped up, and there are many cities and towns where in-migration has produced rapid population growth. Almost always such growth is accompanied by sharply rising land costs, overloaded transportation systems, and a general deterioration of the physical environment. In a number of suburban areas, huge concrete housing projects have been built, and they are often filled by upwardly mobile, well-educated white collar workers. Many of these people look upon such housing as temporary and so do not take an interest in community affairs. Since these newcomers are not socially stratified, they have no "natural" leaders. However, problems that affect their lives—for example, inadequate garbage collection or complaints about the local school situation—generate political activity. Organizations will be formed, and intelligent, and talented individuals who can articulate these complaints will be pressed into leadership of these task-oriented organizations. There is some evidence to suggest that the suburban white collar class can be mobilized by radical politicians. Although the proportion of left-wing mayors throughout the country is still small, it is in these rapidly growing communities that they are most likely to be elected. The conservative Liberal Democratic party still dominates the national political scene, but a pattern of multi-party politics is emerging in some towns and cities. It may well be that the basis for future trends in national politics is being laid in changes occurring at the local level.

4 Business

In 1945 Japan's economic future looked bleak. The nation had suffered defeat in a major war, its cities lay in ruins, its colonial empire was lost, and its foreign markets were closed to Japanese traders. Today Japan is not only the leading industrial power in Asia, but it has surpassed many of the European countries in terms of steel production, shipbuilding capacity, car manufacturing, electronics and other major heavy industry output. Japan's gross national product is third largest in the world, surpassed only by that of the United States and the Soviet Union. Per capita national income, however, is still low, and in 1970 Japan ranked fifth among the nations in the free world with populations of 80 million or more. In any case, the economic recovery within a space of a quarter of a century is sufficiently remarkable to have been given the label of an "economic miracle."

This miracle, of course, was associated with a consistently high economic growth rate. The economy grew because corporations and businessmen invested heavily in modernized production facilities and adopted technical innovations, some of which was imported from the Western nations under licensing arrangements. The economy also grew because there was a pool of skilled labor able and willing to work hard. In short, economic growth was achieved under a capitalistic system of production. But in all this there was also the hand of government. Historically in Japan, business has relied on government for guidance and sundry forms of assistance, and the working relationship between the two continues today.

GOVERNMENT AND THE ECONOMY

The government can affect the activities of business enterprises both indirectly and directly. It can help business by creating an economic climate favorable to business expansion by adopting certain fiscal policies. If the Bank of Japan, the central banking institution, permits expansion of the money supply or if the government undertakes deficit financing, the economy will be stimulated; if the economy gets overheated and inflationary pressures become too strong, it can impose monetary restraints in order to stabilize the situation.

In most of the economically advanced countries, the government undertakes some degree of fiscal management, but in Japan its role is crucial because of the way in which corporations raise the capital necessary for expansion. Capital that comes from profits or from the sale of stock in the corporation is equity capital. Firms may also borrow funds from banks and other lending agencies or sell long-term bonds. American corporations generally have a high equity-to-debt ratio, and even utilities, which traditionally depend heavily on borrowed money, normally have equity equal to 50 percent or more of their total capitalization. By contrast, Japanese corporations have low equity by American standards. Many operate with 4 dollars of borrowed money for every dollar of equity capital. Corporations usually borrow from banks, and as much as one-third of the borrowings may represent short-term loans. The banks in turn get their funds from their depositors, but banks are sometimes known to lend more money than they have on deposit. When they run short, the banks go to the Bank of Japan for credits.

Financial operations of this kind entail a good deal of risk, but the risks can be minimized if there is cooperation among firms, banks, and government. Certain large firms and banks develop close working relationships, and, according to one account, "a group of firms can be relied upon to extend helping hands to a single firm in the group whenever necessary, materially or otherwise, thereby effectively hedging the possibility of failure."[1]

[1] Hideo Kimura, "Financial Policies," in Robert Ballon (ed.), *Doing Business in Japan* (Tokyo: Sophia University–Tuttle, 1967), p. 60.

Finally, faith in the government's willingness to bail them out in the event of serious trouble makes it easier for firms to take the risks necessary to expand business operations. During the 1960s, the era of rapid economic growth, competition among corporations was keen. Each firm sought to increase its share of the market, and the eyes of the management were focused not only on increasing profits, but also on the relative position of the firm within the industry in terms of sales. Hugh Patrick believes that this competitive spirit was an important reason for the large amount of capital investment.[2]

It is not surprising, under the circumstances, that the economy from time to time suffers the consequences of overexpansion, declining profits, bankruptcy of weaker firms, and increasing unemployment. The government then intervenes directly to turn the situation around. For example, in 1964–1965, the stock market declined sharply. In order to shore it up, the Japan Joint Securities Corporation and the Japan Securities Holding Association were formed to step in and buy shares on the open market. Capital for the two organizations came directly from private banks and security companies and from the Bank of Japan.[3]

The government has also intervened in other ways. The Ministry of International Trade and Industry (MITI) is a powerful agency that concerns itself with industrial development and with the state of the nation's foreign trade. The Ministry has consistently pursued a protectionist policy, trying to the best of its ability to keep out foreign imports that would compete with domestic products and to prevent foreign companies, especially American, from getting a foothold in the Japanese economy through large-scale investments in Japan. However, since Japanese firms are selling their wares in foreign markets and investing in foreign countries, the Japanese government is under considerable pressure to liberalize its restrictive policies. Foreign firms and countries, by threatening to close off markets to Japanese goods, are in a strong bargaining position. The automobile

[2] Hugh Patrick, "The Phoenix Risen from the Ashes: Postwar Japan," in James B. Crowley (ed.), *Modern East Asia: Essays in Interpretation* (New York: Harcourt, Brace and World, 1970), p. 319.

[3] Yoshio Terasawa, "Capital Market," in Ballon, *op. cit.*, pp. 110–12.

industry is a case in point. Japanese cars in recent years have become increasingly popular in the United States. The Japanese market, which has been growing rapidly, was closed to American auto manufacturers by restrictions on foreign investments imposed by the Japanese government. These restrictions effectively prevented American manufacturers from establishing assembly plants in Japan. For understandable reasons, Ford, General Motors, and Chrysler executives were openly critical about this restrictive policy, and after several years of pressure from the American side, the Japanese government in the spring of 1971 decided to allow foreign firms to acquire up to 50 percent ownership in Japanese auto and truck manufacturing firms. As a result of this policy of liberalization of capital investments, the major American car manufacturers subsequently purchased minority interest in several Japanese companies. Liberalization in a number of other fields has also been promised.

THE STRUCTURE OF JAPANESE BUSINESS

Whenever the state exercises strong initiative in promoting industrial development, as was the case historically in Japan, economic concentration is likely to result. Prior to World War II, four or five industrial combines known collectively as the *zaibatsu* (money clique) dominated the economy. These huge monopolies were controlled by families through holding companies, which in turn held controlling shares in corporations engaged in banking, insurance, heavy industry, shipping, warehousing, merchandising, publishing, and so on. One of the first tasks of the American reformers in the Occupation was to break up these combines in order to democratize the Japanese economic system. Toward this end, the top holding companies were ordered dissolved, and interlocking directorships were eliminated. The general idea was to break these interrelated firms into independent operating units. The Occupation also had enacted an antimonopoly law, and it created a Fair Trade Commission to enforce it.

Despite these efforts, the goals of the Occupation were not achieved over the long run. Although family control no longer exists, those firms which were part of the old zaibatsu complex are prominent in the economy today. Deconcentration and economic democracy fell victim to the policy of encouraging economic growth. According to Yamamura, government policy stimulated growth, which in turn led to overinvestment and the need to protect against excessive competition. The result was the formation of cartels. "These cartels encouraged further overinvestment which in turn demanded and received more protection."[4] But as we suggested in Chapter 1, huge firms like Toyota and Mitsubishi actually sit atop a pyramid, the base of which is made up of many small firms that are tied to the big corporation through a complex system of subcontracting. Since firms like Toyota are internationally visible, foreigners tend to assume that they typify the Japanese economy, but this is not so.

There are, in addition, small businesses that are not satellites of the giant corporations. In Japan, consumer tastes and habits have persisted along traditional lines to a remarkable degree, so that there is still a domestic market for traditional types of housewares, food products, clothing, and the like which can be met by small firms. Another sector where small businesses persist is retail trade. The residential areas of Japanese towns and cities abound in small shops, each one selling some specialized items—toys, books, tea, electrical goods—and housing the family in back of or above the store.

The general situation of these small business establishments, which account for an important sector of the economy in terms of employment, is not exactly favorable. Wage rates in the small companies are substantially below those paid in the large corporations. Many of the small businessmen lead a precarious existence, and the bankruptcy rate is high, particularly during those periods when the Bank of Japan pursues a tight money policy to check overexpansion. The government is solicitous of the welfare of small and medium-sized businesses, but it has not been able to assist them in a significant way. Owners of small businesses have never been able to exert the kind of influ-

[4] Kozo Yamamura, *Economic Policy in Postwar Japan* (Berkeley, Calif.: University of California Press, 1967), p. 86.

ence, either economically or politically, commensurate with their numerical strength. It is fairly easy to guess why this should be so: They have not been able to organize effectively to make their potential political power felt. Geographically scattered, small businessmen also face intense competition among themselves, as well as with big business. Because many of them operate on a shoestring, their energies are necessarily concentrated on making a living.

The future of many of the small neighborhood retail establishments looks rather grim, given the economies of scale that operate in favor of supermarkets and department stores. As for the subcontracting firms in the industrial sector, their hope, according to one recent study, lies in the attitude of the large corporations: "Where the big company shares the growing belief that small companies exist, not to be exploited, but to be re-organized and re-equipped to increase productivity on a broad front, substantial progress can be made."[5]

BUSINESS ORGANIZATIONS

Historically, the emergence of organizations representing business in Japan may be traced to the years following World War I. Their development, associated with the tremendous expansion that occurred in commerce and industry as a result of the war boom, symbolized the fact that Japanese business had reached maturity.

Today, the most powerful business association is the Federation of Economic Organizations (Keizai Dantai Rengokai or Keidanren). Its lineage goes back to the prewar associations, but it was organized in 1946. The membership consists of the major national trade associations, hundreds of large corporations, and government and quasi-government corporations like the National Railways and Japan Air Lines. Quite clearly, this organization speaks for big business. According to Chitoshi Yanaga, the federation's "primary aim is to create a political

[5] Seymour Broadbridge, *Industrial Dualism in Japan* (Chicago: Aldine, 1966), p. 93.

climate and economic conditions that will insure profits for business and industry through cooperation with the government and within the business community."[6] When the federation takes a public stand on issues or when its officers approach government officials or political party leaders, they not only have easy access; they are likely to be listened to.

Another business group, the Japanese Committee for Economic Development (Keizai Doyukai), was also launched in 1946 by younger corporation executives whose outlook was more progressive than those who led the Federation of Economic Organizations. The membership of the committee is made up of about 1,500 individuals, including the top management officials of some government corporations. The Committee for Economic Development is interested in promoting modern management techniques, in making business more socially responsible, and in reforming democratic politics. It engages in political action as well as research.

A third major business association is the Japanese Chamber of Commerce. The history of the Chamber of Commerce goes back to 1878, when it was founded with government encouragement. It is a federation of local and regional chambers of commerce, and works in many ways to promote business, including foreign trade. Unlike the Federation of Economic Organizations, it includes among its members small and medium-sized firms, and one of its concerns is looking after the welfare of such firms.

The Japanese Federation of Employers Association (Nihon Keieisha Dantai Renmei) membership overlaps with that of the Federation of Economic Organizations, but it includes national and prefectural trade and employers' associations as well as small and medium-sized business establishments. It is primarily concerned with labor problems and seeks to promote management's point of view with respect to labor to the government and the political parties and also to the public through the mass media.

Finally, there are a large number of trade associations that represent the interests of companies engaged in similar kinds

[6] Chitoshi Yanaga, *Big Business in Japanese Politics* (New Haven: Yale University Press, 1968), p. 44.

of industries. The most powerful of these associations, of course, are those representing important national industries such as steel, auto manufacturing, shipbuilding, textiles, and the like.

BUSINESS AND POLITICS

As we have seen, business is in a position to affect inputs into the political system both individually and through its associations. Large corporations, as we shall see in a later chapter, also contribute substantial sums to both individual politicians and the ruling Liberal Democratic party. Business enjoys access to the top administrative and political leadership, and it would be fair to characterize the general political climate as one favorable to business enterprise. But it would not be correct to say that business runs the country.

For one thing, not many businessmen have entered the political arena themselves or taken temporary appointments within the government bureaucracy. The business community has been willing to leave the task of government pretty much up to the bureaucrats and the politicians. Moreover, there is by no means agreement among the business associations as to their proper role vis-à-vis government. For instance, the Federation of Economic Organizations is much less willing to intervene directly and openly in politics than, say, the Committee on Economic Development.[7] "Business," according to one study, "has won a greater right to be consulted, but it has avoided anything in the nature of a confrontation with the politicians. Still, it makes the attempt to guide national economic policy on an organized scale through the associations and other channels of influence."[8] Finally, the breakup of the prewar family-controlled zaibatsu has resulted in more pluralism within business. On many issues, business is likely to speak out with many voices rather than one.

In general, Japanese business is much more willing to accept

[7] A. J. Heidenheimer and F. C. Langdon, *Business Associations and the Financing of Political Parties* (The Hague: Martinus Nijihoff, 1968), p. 193.
[8] *Ibid.*, p. 200.

government direction (or interference, depending on one's point of view) than American business. To begin with, there is no tradition of laissez-faire economics. The government played a role in Japan's economic development historically and continues to influence the economic state of the country through its fiscal policy, its encouragement of mergers, and so on. Furthermore, when the government, in seeking to enhance Japan's competitive position in the world economy, intervenes in such matters as mergers, import restrictions, and limitations on foreign investments, business firms appear to be willing to subordinate their concern to maximize their own profits to the larger national interest—that is, the health of the Japanese economy as a whole.

5 Labor

The emergence of a capitalist economy and the growth of industry on a substantial scale have brought about changes in virtually every sector of Japanese life. Of these changes, one of the most important has been the creation of a working class owning little or no property and dependent upon wages for its livelihood. The creation of such a class can, at least potentially, bring about far-reaching modifications in the political structure. Since the mode of life and economic interests of workers presumably are different from those of other groups such as the peasantry and the business class, their political attitudes too should be different. And if all workers could unite behind a single political program, they could become a potent political force.

Partly because of the encouragement given it by the Occupation, Japanese labor has acquired in the postwar period more power than it ever had before. Nevertheless, the position of labor in the overall political picture is still a minor one, and it has not won political victories in keeping with its potential strength. It is pertinent to inquire why Japanese labor should be relatively so weak.

THE LABOR MOVEMENT

Historically, the Japanese labor movement began around the turn of the century. The movement was started by a small group of intellectuals of middle-class origin who were attracted to socialist doctrines. Organized labor remained small and ineffectual, and although it began to grow after the end of World War I, it never became a major force in either economic or political affairs. In 1936, the peak year, trade union membership stood at 420,000 and represented only 6.9 percent of nonagricultural workers. After 1936 and until the close of World War II, union membership and activity declined, owing, among other things, to government suppression.

The social and political environment for labor changed dramatically under the Occupation, which at first openly favored a strong, healthy labor movement on the premise that it could contribute to the growth of political democracy. This meant that union leaders were now no longer on the defensive, but had the backing of the highest political authority. The intellectual and social ferment of this period, which forced many people to question the validity and usefulness of old ideas and institutions, also provided a background favorable to the growth of trade unions. Within a short time, unions sprang up almost everywhere. In some instances, old-line leaders reemerged; in others, enthusiastic young men without previous experience in the labor movement pushed forward to establish unions. There were even cases where unions were formed at the suggestion of employers, the idea being that if the formation of unions was inevitable, it would be better to have them led by men who were fundamentally friendly to the employer.

The number of workers who could be brought into the unions has grown steadily over the years. Table 3 shows the breakdown of the total work force in the 1960s.

Table 3: Total Working Force and Those in Manufacturing and Services (in millions)

Year	Total Force	Manufacturing	Services
1960	44.61	9.51	6.80
1969	50.40	13.45	8.78

Source: International Labour Office, *Year Book of Labour Statistics*, 1970 edition, p. 317.

As can be seen, between 1960 and 1969 men and women in manufacturing and service industries, which are prime targets for unionization, increased by 5.92 million, which is more than the 5.79 million increase in the total working force.

Union membership, of course, has grown. In 1955 just under 6.3 million workers were in unions, while by 1970 the figure had jumped to 11.6 million. The percentage of workers in unions, however, has remained remarkably stable, varying between 35 and 37 percent. The Japanese rate of unionization is less than the rate in Great Britain, about equal to West Germany's, and higher than the American rate.

Not all industries are unionized to an equal degree. In 1967, just over 70 percent of government workers were unionized, followed by 67.5 percent of workers in transportation and communications, electricity, gas and water, and 66.3 percent of mine workers. The lowest rates were found in fisheries, retail trade, finance, insurance, and real estate, where less than 1 out of 5 were enrolled in a union.[1]

The rate of unionization also varies according to the size of the plant or factory. Unions are most likely to be found in the large modern plants employing 1,000 or more workers, while they have not been organized in the small family-operated backalley workshops. In 1970, for example, a little more than 58 percent of union members employed in the private sector were working in enterprises with 1,000 or more workers.[2]

These statistics tell us something about the magnitude of organized labor in Japan, and give us an inkling about its potential as a political force. But unless one probes a little deeper, he is likely to misjudge the power labor is able to exert in the political arena. Labor is weaker than it might be, and the chief cause, it would appear, lies in its fragmentation.

THE FRAGMENTATION OF LABOR

Labor does not speak as one voice and act as one unit. One cause is the way in which unions are organized. An unusual

[1] Ohara Shakai Mondai Kenkyujo, *Nihon Rodo Nenkan* [Japan Labor Yearbook], (Tokyo, 1969), p. 196.

[2] *Japan Labor Bulletin,* 10, 3 (March 1971), 5.

feature of organized labor in Japan is the preponderant position occupied by "enterprise" unions. As the name implies, an enterprise union is one in which all employees of a mine, shop, or factory—or of a company that owns several factories, including clerical and even some supervisory employees—come together to form one union. In the case of very large plants, there may be more than one union.

The preference for enterprise rather than the industrial unions more typical of many advanced countries is probably related to the employment practices that prevail in Japan. Something like 35 percent of the employees in large firms are given permanent tenure with remuneration based on seniority and educational attainment. In such an arrangement, a young man just out of high school is hired and then given specialized training by the company. If he works out, he acquires permanent status, and the expectation is that he will stay with that firm until he retires. Most union members consist of such permanent employees. In addition, firms employ many temporary workers who do not enjoy job security, and they usually do not belong to the union. Thus union members represent the elite of the working class.

Since pay is based on seniority, the younger workers, who are often more productive because they have been trained more recently in the latest production techniques, are underpaid. In the long run things will even out, since their pay will increase as they get older, but many younger workers are restive. They are consumption-oriented and want their rewards now rather than later. Managers are meeting this problem in typical Japanese fashion by giving additional pay to those with technical skills, but not giving them line authority.

In a situation in which an employee has a lifetime commitment to a firm, he tends to develop loyalty to the company. He wants to see his firm emerge as a leader within that particular industry, and perhaps more important, he sees his personal welfare tied to the employer's ability to maintain a high level of profits. Japanese firms, moreover, are highly paternalistic. In addition to the basic wage, workers are paid semi-annual bonuses, given family allowances and other extras, may have access to company-owned housing, and can spend their vacations at company-owned resorts. As a result, many workers develop what some Japanese observers have called "dual allegiance," that is, loyalty to the company as well as to the union.

Because of the high economic growth rate as well as the marked slowdown in population growth, Japan, like some European countries, has experienced a labor shortage in recent years. This in turn has increased the bargaining power of labor. Wage rates have risen sharply, until today the Japanese wage level, although much lower than the American, is substantially above those that prevail in other parts of Asia. Thus, we find a pattern that is in many ways similar to what has taken place in the West. As the country has become more industrialized, its per capita income has risen. Wages are higher, people have more money to spend—the age of mass consumption has arrived. A mass consumption culture, moreover, tends to have a leveling effect; the life styles of blue collar workers today are not all that much different from those of the middle class. Status distinctions in plants and factories have also become blurred with the emergence of a "gray collar" class of highly skilled workers who operate sophisticated machines. The lower ranks of the white collar class now blend into the upper ranks of the blue collar class. Under these circumstances, there has been a noticeable tendency for workers to identify with the middle class, and surveys suggest that well over half of union members think of themselves as belonging to the middle class. This identification has changed individual value orientations, and today workers tend to be more interested in personal hobbies, recreation, and family life—the sorts of concerns that used to be typical of the white collar class. Japanese workers, at least those that are skilled and working in large modern plants, are becoming more "bourgeois" in their outlook.

NATIONAL FEDERATIONS

As we mentioned above, the basic union is the enterprise union. Some are independent; others are affiliated with national unions. Some of the national unions in turn are affiliated with large national federations. Unions may also change their affiliations. This is particularly a problem when two firms whose unions are affiliated with different national unions or federations merge. In fact, proposed mergers have occasionally been called off because of opposition from unions affiliated with different federations.

There were, as of 1970, three major national federations. The largest is the General Council of Trade Unions of Japan (Nihon Rodo Kumiai Sohyo Kaigi or Sohyo). Its membership totaled 4,260,000, or almost 38 percent of the national total. Sohyo was founded in 1950 with the encouragement of the Occupation, which was interested in purging the labor movement of Communist leadership. Ironically, it subsequently turned to the Left and has been one of the most active of those organizations opposing the alliance with the United States. At the national level, Sohyo pursues both economic and political objectives. Almost every year, labor launches a "spring offensive" to seek wage raises as well as better fringe benefits, such as more holidays, increased severance pay, compensation insurance for injuries, and so on. Interspersed with economic demands are political demands. In recent years, for example, Sohyo has consistently opposed the entry of American nuclear warships into Japanese harbors, American military actions in Southeast Asia, and the strengthening of the Japanese Self-Defense Forces. In general, it is highly critical of the existing capitalistic system and seeks to replace it with a socialist order.

However, it is worth remembering that neither Sohyo nor the other labor federations are cohesive, monolithic organizations. Like most large-scale organizations in Japan, the federation is composed of several factions that try to stay together to achieve common ends. From time to time the composition of the top leadership changes as the outcome of factional strife; when this occurs, one can expect some shifts in policy positions.

The second largest federation is the Japanese Confederation of Labor (Zen Nihon Rodo Sodomei or Domei), with 1,962,000 members, or about 17 percent of the membership of organized labor. In terms of policy position, Domei is much more moderate than Sohyo and seeks to improve the economic position of labor by working within the capitalist system.

The third major group is the Federation of Independent Unions (Churitsu Rodokumiai Renraku Kaigi or Churitsuroren), which claims 1,344,000 members or about 12 percent of the membership. The fourth large national organization is the National Federation of Industrial Organizations (Zenkoku Sangyobetsu Rodokumiai Rengo or Shinsanbetsu), with a membership of less than 100,000. In addition, there are a number of unions and smaller federations that are not affiliated with the national federations. In 1970 these unaffiliated unions accounted for almost 3.5 million workers or about one-third of all organized labor.

The three large national federations present some differences in terms of their constituent unions. Table 4 gives the affiliation of the 12 largest unions (as of 1970).

Table 4: Twelve Largest Unions (1970) According to Affiliation and Sector (no. of members in parentheses)

Union	Public Sector	Private Sector
General Council (Sohyo)		
All-Japan Prefectural and Municipal Workers (892,888)	x	
Japan Teachers Union (564,234)	x	
National Railway Workers (270,183)	x	
General Federation of Private Railway Workers (248,757)		x
Joint Council of Telecommunications Workers (265,194)	x	
All-Japan Postal Workers (233,304)	x	
National Trade Union of Metal and Engineering Workers (224,394)		x
Japanese Federation of Iron and Steel Workers (210,288)		x
Confederation (Domei)		
Japanese Federation of Textile Workers (548,361)		x
National Federation of Metal Industry Trade Union (278,582)		x
Federation of Independent Unions (Churitsuroren)		
All-Japan Federation of Electric Machine Workers (535,908)		x
National Federation of Life Insurance Workers (265,048)		x
National Federation of Construction Workers (256,567)		x

As Table 4 reveals, the largest unions within Sohyo tend to be in the public sector rather than the private, the opposite of the other two federations. Government workers and those employed in government corporations like the National Railways are politically militant because (1) their right to strike is restricted by legislation, and (2) where the government is the employer, the best way to bring pressure to improve working conditions is through political means. For example, since railway employees are forbidden to strike, they express their grievances by resorting to such methods as observing safety regulations so strictly that train schedules cannot be met, causing traffic tieups and massive delays. The government then finds it difficult to discipline such workers—they have not, after all, broken any law.

UNIONS AND LEFT-WING PARTIES

From the very beginning of the labor movement, it has had close ties with the Socialist party. As we mentioned earlier, the first labor unions were organized by Japanese Socialists at the turn of the present century. Since then, Socialists (and also Communists) have actively sought the support of labor unions, and union leaders in turn have identified themselves with the Left.

In recent years, Sohyo has consistently supported the Socialist party by providing funds, especially during elections, by mobilizing votes, and by putting up candidates for elective offices at various levels—local, prefectural, and national. For example, in the 1969 election for the House of Representatives, 40 out of 90 successful Socialist party candidates had union endorsement. The other large national federation, Domei, has supported the rival Democratic Socialist party. In the 1969 election, 7 out of 31 successful Democratic Socialist Diet members were endorsed by Domei.

The identification of labor unions with the Socialist and the Democratic Socialist parties, however, is not without its drawbacks. For one thing, even though the leaders of a federation may throw their support to one party, there is no assurance that the rank and file will necessarily follow. As many as 1 out of 4 workers in large-scale enterprises identify with the conservative

Liberal Democratic party, while another 20 percent or so do not identify with any party, either because they feel none of the parties is worth supporting, or because they are apathetic and indifferent to politics.[3] Labor's open support of the Socialist and Democratic Socialist parties, moreover, tends to hinder its access to the government through the ruling Liberal Democratic party. By being consistently anti-Establishment, so to speak, labor loses its ability to affect significant inputs into the political system.

From time to time, labor leaders have come out in favor of separating the labor movement from left-wing party politics. Labor unions, so the view goes, should concentrate on striving to improve working conditions and should remain neutral insofar as politics are concerned. A recent example is the suggestion put forward in the spring of 1970 by leaders of unions in the private sector affiliated with Sohyo. Their suggestion was that the federation should cease giving exclusive support to the Socialist party. In a related move, a Council of Chairmen of Large Unions in the Private Sector was established to try to unify the labor movement by cutting across the three major national federations. It is difficult to see how this new organization can truly unify the labor movement, since it seems to exclude the powerful unions in the public sector—for instance, schoolteachers, national railroad workers, and so on. Instead of labor movement unity, it might result in greater fragmentation.

Although there are obvious advantages to be gained from breaking organized labor's affiliation with political parties and the preoccupation of the major federations with political problems, it does not seem likely that labor will move in this direction. First, despite the rise of organized labor in the postwar period, power within the Diet and in the government generally has been in the hands of conservative political forces basically hostile to labor. Under the circumstances, the tendency is for labor to look upon any government action with suspicion; and labor will probably never feel fully secure until it has managed to attain more political power than it has to date. Second, many

[3] Tokeisuri Kenkyujo, *Kokumin-sei no Kenkyu* [Study of National Character] (Tokyo, 1968), p. 143.

important economic questions are intimately related to political decisions. Taxation and inflation, to mention two, directly affect the economic position of labor, yet both belong fundamentally to the political sphere. Third, as we have already mentioned, many of the big employers are government corporations immune to economic actions such as strikes; hence they must be moved through political action. For these and other reasons, Japanese labor is not likely to leave the political arena.

Having said this, one must add that in the long run the political role of unions is likely to undergo some subtle changes. Without question, the support given by trade union members to the Socialist party declined in the decade of the 1960s. For example, one survey shows that among members of the Japanese Federation of Iron and Steel Workers Union, about 72 percent supported the Socialist party in 1960; by 1969, the figure had dropped to about 23 percent. This may be a somewhat extreme case, but the same trend is found in many unions, and is very likely a function of the growing identification of workers with the middle class.

Such a shift in class identification, however, does not mean that workers no longer feel they need unions; rather, many workers are increasingly dissatisfied with the way unions have been operating and wish to see them shift their emphases in other directions. Although questions of wages and hours are still important, workers want to see their unions moving actively into other areas—into housing, social security, pollution control, holidays, vacations, and recreational facilities. That is, they want attention to the problems of leisure as well as of work. Workers also want their unions to involve themselves in worker training, placement, promotion, and merit evaluation.

This concern with personal matters may well be related to the growing alienation of union labor toward their tasks in the factory. The large-scale use of automated machinery and the organization of production on an assembly-line basis has made factory work boring, and many Japanese workers, like workers in the United States and other industrialized nations, suffer from low morale and lack of positive motivation. Japanese workers not only want the unions to be concerned with these problems, but they are pressuring the leadership to let them participate more actively in union affairs. This is particularly true of the younger workers. Indeed, there are signs that the leaders are responding to the pressure from below. During the 1971 "spring offensive," for example, several unions installed television sets in places like employees' dining rooms so that information about the progress of collective bargaining sessions could be conveyed quickly to the members.

6 Agriculture

Historically, Japanese farmers, like their counterparts in many lands, were placed in a disadvantaged position. Compared to their city cousins, they were compelled to work harder and longer hours, endure a lower standard of living, and lead more humdrum lives. Long ago they were sometimes compared to sesame seeds, which, it was said, gave more oil the harder they were squeezed. Today the lot of the farmer may still leave much to be desired, as is evidenced by the observation that many girls do not wish to marry farmers and that many young men and women head for the cities as they reach maturity. Nevertheless, in recent years, farmers, like almost everyone else, have improved their economic status. Part of the reason is that they have been able to use the power of the vote effectively.

AGRICULTURE IN THE NATIONAL ECONOMY

The proportion of the population engaged in agriculture fell to below 50 percent of the total work force, a critical point, in the mid-1920s, much later than in some countries of Western Europe. Since then, the drop in the agricultural population has been precipitous. The high economic growth rate of the 1960s was made possible by large-scale migration from the rural areas into the cities. In 1950 about 53 percent of the middle and high school graduates went into farming, whereas by 1965 the figure had dropped to just under 5 percent. Stated another way, agriculture has been supplying between 600,000 and 800,000 workers for industry every year. This means that the rural areas have borne the cost of educating the younger generation only to have them leave, thus depriving the countryside of their productive capacity. In this sense, the farmers have been subsidizing the growth of industry.

Incidentally, urban migration has not been distributed evenly over the entire country. The areas that have attracted migrants are the large cities located in a belt extending westward from Tokyo to Nagoya, the Inland Sea, and into northern Kyushu. According to projections, about 60 million people or 54 percent of the population will be living in this belt by 1980.

The migration from the farm areas has, of course, affected the structure of agriculture. The shift from full- to part-time farming is continuing, as Table 5 shows.

Table 5: Full- and Part-time Farm Households (in millions)

Year	Total Farm Households	Farm is Sole Source of Income	Farm is Major Source of Income	Farm is not Major Source of Income
1965	5.66	1.22	2.08	2.36
1970	5.34	0.83	1.80	2.71

Source: Compiled from data in *Japan Report*, vol. 17, no. 2 (January 16, 1971), p. 6. Published by the Consulate General of Japan, New York.

In many families, the male head has taken a job in a nearby factory and commutes from his farm. This is feasible, since about 60 percent of the rural communities are within a 10-minute walking distance from a railway station or bus stop. In other families, the father goes to work in a big city for months at a time, leaving the farm chores to the wife, children, and grandparents. By contrast, other farmers who have chosen to be full-time operators have gone in for a more commercialized type of agriculture, and have turned to more mechanization and more scientific farm management. This trend is reflected in the growth in the number of larger farms and a decline in the small farms.

The interesting thing is that despite the reduction in the

number of full-time farm households, agricultural production has held up remarkably well. Industrialized as Japan is, more than 80 percent of the total domestic demand for foodstuffs was met by home production in 1969. In the case of rice, Japan has been plagued by a surplus that has forced the government-held stockpile to increase markedly. As a result, the government has compelled cutbacks in rice production and encouraged the conversion of paddy fields into farm land suitable for other crops. As they grow more affluent, the Japanese are eating less rice and more wheat, meat, fruits, and vegetables.

Since agricultural production has been holding up while farm population has dropped, incomes from farm operations have risen somewhat. The largest increase in incomes, however, has been accounted for by nonagricultural income earned by farmers who have taken jobs in industry. In 1968, side businesses and part-time employment produced something like 37 percent of the average income of farming families. Thanks to their rising incomes, farmers can now afford many of the amenities of life previously enjoyed only by city workers. Today the rate of car ownership among farm families does not differ much from that of urban working families. Similarly, the proportion of children going on to high school is almost the same as that found in the cities.

FARM ORGANIZATIONS

Farmers, like businessmen and workers, have organizations to promote their economic interests. The first such organization, the Imperial Agricultural Association, was founded in the 1870s under government leadership. It was followed by rural cooperatives, also established on government initiative to help small farmers by supplying them with credit. The basic legislation regarding cooperatives was enacted in 1900. Both the Imperial Agricultural Association and the cooperatives tended to be under the influence of the landlord class.

It was inevitable that sooner or later organizations representing the lower social strata in the rural areas would emerge. After World War I, the Japan Farmer's Union was founded by

Christian Socialists, and hundreds of local tenant unions affiliated with it.

During World War II, all farm groups were forced by the government to merge into an officially sponsored Agricultural Association. Under the Occupation, farm organizations that traced their lineage to the early groups re-formed. The left-wing Japan Farmer's Union (Nihon Nomin Kumiai or Nichino), for example, was organized by the Socialists in 1946, and its campaign to organize tenant farmers was quite successful. The Nichino was particularly active in those areas which had been the scene of tenant disputes before the war, and in many instances it took the lead in pushing through the Occupation-sponsored land reform program by giving advice to tenant farmers, by getting its members elected to the local land commissions that implemented land reform, and by running its men in local elections.

For several years Nichino managed to ride the crest of the wave of change that swept over the rural areas as a result of the land reform, but beginning about 1948, its popularity rapidly waned. One reason for its decline was the struggle between the Socialists and the Communists within the organization. Another and perhaps more fundamental reason was that the chief plank in its program—land for the landless—lost its appeal once many tenant farmers got land as a result of the land reform program. At present, the All-Japan Federation of Farmer's Unions (Zen-Nihon Nomin Kumiai Rengokai or Zen-Nichino), the successor to the Japan Farmer's Union, is the largest of several left-wing groups, but it is overshadowed by the Agricultural Cooperative Association.

The Agricultural Cooperative Association was established by law in 1947 and may be regarded as a successor to the wartime Agricultural Association. Today it is the largest farm organization in the country and wields considerable economic and political power. The basic unit of the cooperative association is the hamlet or village cooperative, of which there are some 10,000 located in every part of the country. One noteworthy feature is that the local units are based on geography (for instance, a village), rather than along functional lines such as the sale of farm products (note the parallel with enterprise unions). Moreover, most coops have an unusually high rate of participation, and almost every family in a village will belong. It is reported that about 93 percent of all farm families belong to the local cooperatives. Another characteristic of these coops is that they are engaged in a number of activities important to farm families. The cooperatives are involved in the sale of agricultural products, in the purchasing of items frequently used in farming operations, in taking in savings and providing credit, and in selling insurance. In addition, the coop may take the lead in introducing new agricultural techniques, and generally in providing leadership in the rural communities.

The village-level cooperatives are affiliated with the prefectural cooperative organization. The prefectural cooperatives, in turn, are affiliated with the national cooperative headquarters in Tokyo. Thus the Agricultural Cooperative Association represents a pyramid of coops resting on a base consisting of 10,000 hamlet or village units. Ostensibly, its primary function is to provide for the economic needs of farmers; it is not primarily a political organization. The Association itself states publicly that it is "politically neutral." But it would be naive to suppose that such is the case.

To begin with, the Agricultural Cooperative Association was established by law, and under the terms of subsequent legislation, both the national and prefectural headquarters organizations receive annual subsidies from the government. The subsidy, which for the national headquarters amounts to less than 10 percent of its income, is not so significant from the financial point of view. Symbolically, however, it confirms the public character of the organization. The close ties with the government are also suggested by the type of men who have attained top leadership positions. Its first president had previously held the post of vice minister of agriculture. He was succeeded by an individual who had headed the Nagano prefectural headquarters, while the third president of the association was a person who had previously been a member of the House of Councillors and of the Liberal Democratic party.

Probably the most important link with the government concerns the role of the cooperative association in the distribution of rice, the staple crop. During the war and in the early postwar era, rice was rationed because it was in short supply. The government purchased rice from the producers and sold it to the consumers. Today there is no need to ration rice because there is a surplus, but the government continues to be involved in rice distribution in order to maintain prices at a high level. What happens is that the government buys the rice from farmers at a higher price than would be achieved by supply and demand and sells it to urban consumers at a lower price than it paid. The deficit, of course, is made up from general tax funds. In short, farmers are receiving a subsidy.

In making its rice purchases, the government utilizes the cooperatives. The coops are paid a fee based on the number of sacks of rice handled. Moreover, a lump-sum payment is made to the central agricultural cooperative bank, which in turn distributes the money to the local cooperatives who then credit the account of each farmer who sold rice. The cooperative association in a sense acts as the agent of the government and benefits financially from this activity.

FARMERS IN POLITICS

If the Agricultural Cooperative Association acts as an agent of the government, it also plays a somewhat contradictory role—namely, that of a pressure group. Every summer the government must set the price it is willing to pay for the rice it will purchase. The interests of the government and the rice producers naturally conflict: One party wants the price as low as possible; the other, as high as possible. The stage is set for bargaining between the two parties, the farmers being represented by the cooperative association, which will suggest a price.

To strengthen its bargaining position, the cooperative association every year engages in what has come to be known as the "human sea strategy." Literally waves of farmers descend on the government agencies and on the members of the Liberal Democratic party for the purpose of applying pressure to have the price of rice set at a high level. The cooperatives mobilize their members by paying their fare to Tokyo and giving them a per diem in order to overwhelm opposition by sheer weight of numbers. When they circulate petitions, they may have secured as many as 4 million signatures. When they schedule mass meetings on an appointed day throughout the country, they may have gotten out as many as 150,000 farmers. The delegations to Tokyo call on individual Diet members elected from predominantly rural districts, and in this way bring pressure to bear on the Liberal Democratic party. Finally, they even engage in sit-ins. Observers liken the cooperatives' campaign every summer to the annual "spring offensives" of organized labor. The difference appears to be that farmers generally carry more political clout because they support the ruling party with their votes.

One can cite other examples of the power of farmers. The Occupation-sponsored land reform program begun in 1946 compelled landlords to sell their holdings in excess of the amount allowed by law (about 7.3 acres) to the state, which in turn sold the land to tenant farmers. More than 4.5 million acres of land changed hands in this way. As compensation, landlords were given long-term government bonds. The problem, however, was that rapid inflation in subsequent years wiped out much of the purchasing power of the bonds. To make matters worse, from the point of view of the landlords, land which was sold cheaply at 1946 prices appreciated tremendously in value, especially farm land that happened to be located on the fringes of cities. Many tenant farmers eventually sold farm land they had acquired during the land reform as industrial sites or as residential subdivisions, and became very rich in the process.

The landlords understandably felt they had been treated unfairly, and sought compensation from the state. Several hundred suits were filed in the courts on the argument that the land reform was unconstitutional because it took private property without just compensation. In 1953 the Supreme Court put an end to these suits by upholding the constitutionality of the land reform program.

Having been defeated in the courts, the former landlords formed a national organization called the National Farmland League and worked for compensation through political action. Initially, both the Ministry of Agriculture and the Ministry of Finance were hostile to the idea. The Ministry of Agriculture is generally sensitive to agrarian demands, but in this case it was reluctant to help the ex-landlords because it had been the agency which had carried out the land reform. To now favor compensation would be tantamount to admitting that the land reform had been a mistake. In other words, face was involved. The Ministry of Finance resisted for the simple reason that it would have to find the money if compensation was agreed upon. The response of the top leadership of the Liberal Democratic party was also negative. The presumption is that they were reflecting the views of the bureaucrats in the Ministry of Agriculture and the Ministry of Finance.

Despite such powerful opposition, the former landlords were finally able to get legislation passed (in 1965) which authorized payment over a ten-year period to 1,670,000 former landlords and their relatives who had lost land during the land reform. They were successful because through their organization they were able to convince enough Liberal Democratic back benchers that if they did not cooperate, they would face possible defeat in elections. As Fukui puts it, "whatever success the League achieved resulted, in the final analysis, largely from the widely shared belief that it controlled a sizable bloc of votes and therefore was in a position to influence seriously the results of an election."[1] When enough rank-and-file Diet members in the Liberal Democratic party became apprehensive, they in turn applied pressure on the party leadership to change their stand and put through the necessary legislation.

It is curious that despite such evidence of considerable political influence, the farmer's perception of his role in the political system seems to be one of relative powerlessness. In one survey in 1963 in which villagers were asked, "Are farmers' interests and wishes sufficiently reflected in politics?" more than half replied in the negative.[2] Moreover, very few of the Liberal Democratic party supporters who were inter-

[1] Haruhiro Fukui, *Party in Power: The Japanese Liberal-Democrats and Policy-making* (Berkeley, Calif.: University of California Press, 1970), pp. 192–93. The account of the landlord compensation case is drawn from Fukui's book.

[2] Naikaku Chosashitsu, *Noson Shakai no Kozo Henka to Nomin Ishiki no Doko* [Changes in Social Structure in Farming Areas and Trends in the Political Consciousness of Farmers] (Tokyo, 1963), p. 113.

viewed said that they supported the party because of its farm policy. In fact, they were unable to give specific reasons why they favored the Liberal Democrats. This is probably because Japanese peasants, like French peasants, do not approach politics in partisan terms.[3] Values that are stressed in rural areas—social harmony, community solidarity, and consensus—are not conducive to the development of politics based on group or class conflict. Since the Liberal Democratic party stands for traditional conservatism, the nonpartisan or even antipartisan traditionalist ends up being a supporter of that party.

As for the farmers' relative lack of feelings of political competence, we may speculate that it is probably related to the disadvantaged position they have had over a long time when compared to their city cousins. As we have seen, the economic status of agriculturalists has risen both in absolute and in relative terms, but they still feel they are not as well off as city dwellers. The out-migration of young people, increased opportunities for industrial employment, and more mechanization on the farms have had beneficial effects, but it must be recognized that agriculture simply cannot take advantage of the economies of scale that are available to industry. So long as agriculture continues to be operated on a small scale, its overall position relative to that of industry is bound to decline in the long run.

[3] See Sidney Tarrow, "The Urban-rural Cleavage in Political Involvement: The Case of France," *American Political Science Review,* 65, 2 (June 1971), 341–57.

7 The Bureaucracy

"All realistic study of government," says Friedrich, "has to start with an understanding of bureaucracy (or whatever else one prefers to call it), because no government can function without it."[1] Indeed, it may be said that bureaucracy forms the core of modern government. Because of its central position, the bureaucracy performs such a multitude of functions that it is difficult to generalize about its activities. But as Almond and Powell suggest, its peculiar role is concerned with the "outputs" of the political system: "We would like to argue the thesis that bureaucracies tend to monopolize output. Only bureaucrats enforce laws, policies, or decisions."[2]

The bureaucracy has occupied an especially strategic position in Japan's political system. In prewar days, civil servants were responsible to the emperor, and since the emperor in theory could do no wrong, by extension bureaucrats enjoyed an aura of infallibility. Moreover, Japanese bureaucrats have never been hampered by a set of values which holds that the less there is of government, the better; Japan has no laissez-faire legacy. On the contrary, ever since the Meiji Restoration (and even prior to it), the people have had a habit of looking to a paternalistic government for leadership and assistance.

The bureaucracy played a particularly important role in national development during the latter part of the nineteenth

[1] Carl J. Friedrich, *Constitutional Government and Democracy* (Boston: Little, Brown, 1941), p. 57.

[2] Gabriel A. Almond and G. Bing Powell, Jr., *Comparative Politics: A Developmental Approach* (Boston: Little, Brown, 1966), p. 153.

century. Nettl argues that "Japan is the first historical example of developmental nationalism, a value system for which the bureaucracy helped to mobilize commitment."[3] And even today, the bureaucrats represent the major ruling force in Japanese politics.

SIZE AND STRUCTURE

In recent years, roughly 1 out of 12 persons has been employed either by the central government or by local government entities. Of course, a great many of these persons have been employed by government corporations; the bureaucracy in the sense that we are using the term in this chapter is much smaller, and numbers somewhere in the neighborhood of 800,000 to 900,000 individuals.

There are at present (1971), twelve ministries: Justice, Foreign Affairs, Finance, Education, Welfare, Agriculture and Forestry, International Trade and Industry, Transportation, Postal Services, Labor, Construction, and Local Autonomy. In addition, there is a catchall organization, the Office of the Prime Minister, which, although not called a ministry, has important functions. Because of its controversial position, the Defense Agency is not an independent ministry but is part of the Office of the Prime Minister, as is the police. Some of the other important agencies under the jurisdiction of the Office of the Prime Minister are the Personnel Bureau, the Cabinet Legislation Bureau, the Administrative Management Agency, the Fair Trade Commission, the Economic Planning Agency, and the Science and Technology Agency.

In addition to the minister, who is a member of the cabinet, each ministry has parliamentary vice-ministers and an administrative vice-minister, as well as a secretariat. The operating units are the various bureaus or divisions, which are subdivided into sections. Most of the ministries also maintain field offices in all parts of the country, and there is frequent movement of

[3] J. P. Nettl, *Political Mobilization: A Sociological Analysis of Methods and Concepts* (New York: Basic Books, 1967), pp. 374–75.

officials from Tokyo to the field and back. There is less shifting of personnel from one ministry to another. As in business, there is a tendency for an individual to stay with one organization throughout his career.

In Japan as in other advanced countries, the complexity of the problems demanding solutions has led to a proliferation of specialized government agencies and commissions. Hundreds of commissions, with a total membership of thousands, have been set up to advise the government. They usually consist of officials from the ministry or agency most concerned, retired bureaucrats, Diet members, businessmen, scholars, and labor union officials—a membership distribution chosen to represent the economic interests directly involved and the public interest as well. In the course of their work, these commissions often hold public hearings and then submit reports and recommendations, which may or may not be adopted. One of the general purposes of these commissions is to try to bring about some kind of accommodation among the various interests involved in order to make the work of the ministry or agency that much easier.

WHO ARE THE BUREAUCRATS?

The personnel of the early Meiji regime was determined largely by historical circumstances, for it was inevitable that the first bureaucrats would be drawn from among those who had been active in overthrowing the Tokugawa Shogunate. The roster of government personnel therefore included a strong representation of lower samurai, with a sprinkling of court nobles. In terms of geographical origins, officials from the old fiefs of Choshu, Satsuma, Tosa, and Hizen predominated.

With the passage of years, however, the need for a new system of recruitment became apparent. Late in the nineteenth century, a civil service system based on competitive examinations was adopted. Appointments were also made to the middle ranks on the basis of "screening," and the top ranks (cabinet ministers, ambassadors, and so on) fell in the "free appointment" category; that is, they were outside the examination system. The political parties made sporadic attempts to open the civil service to political appointees, but the spoils system was never allowed to take hold.

Spaulding's detailed study of the history of the examination system shows a high failure rate; depending on the year, only 5 to 15 percent of those taking the examinations were successful.[4] There is also little evidence of fraud or favoritism. In Spaulding's judgment:

> Requiring rigorous verification of superior scholastic achievement provided the civil service with a continuing but controlled infusion of young men of proven intellectual capacity. Substituting education for class, regional, and family ties as the indispensable qualification for the inner elite made recruitment much more impersonal than ever before and therefore less vulnerable to favoritism and corruption.[5]

The use of the higher civil service examination system undoubtedly stimulated the development of university education and of a complementary relationship between the examinations and the curriculum of the various law faculties, which were the principal training grounds for civil service aspirants. Not all universities were equally successful in getting their graduates into the civil service. The government-supported institutions generally did better, and one in particular, Tokyo University, was preeminent. To this day, graduates of Tokyo University are disproportionately numerous within the bureaucracy. Kubota, who analyzed a sample of civil servants in office between 1949 and 1959, found that 92.4 percent came from the government-supported institutions, with Tokyo University accounting for 79.0 percent of the total.[6] (He also found that Tokyo graduates were promoted more rapidly.)[7] In terms of educational background, the recruitment base for bureaucrats is thus rather narrow.

From what social strata are Tokyo University students re-

[4] Robert M. Spaulding, *Imperial Japan's Higher Civil Service Examinations* (Princeton, N.J.: Princeton University Press, 1967).
[5] *Ibid*., p. 323.
[6] Akira Kubota, *Higher Civil Servants in Postwar Japan* (Princeton, N.J.: Princeton University Press, 1969), p. 69.
[7] *Ibid*., p. 133.

cruited? Roughly 60 percent of the families of recent Tokyo University students derive their incomes from salaries and wages. Some 40 percent of the students depend on their parents for all their educational expenses, while the majority rely on scholarships and/or part-time work. This is economically possible because Tokyo University, being a tax-supported institution, charges only nominal tuition. Thus, it is clear that Tokyo University by no means caters to children of elite families and that, broadly speaking, it draws individuals from all classes, excluding probably only the very lowest, and propels them into elite positions. Since Tokyo University not only provides many of the bureaucratic elite, but also of the business elite, we can say that there is a meritocracy rather than an aristocracy in Japan.[8]

THE WAYS OF THE BUREAUCRACY

Officialdom and the Public. The relationship between bureaucracy and people in Japan is sometimes described with an old phrase, *kanson mimpi,* which translated literally means, "official exalted—people despised." Before the war, civil officials owed their loyalty and allegiance to the emperor. Each official was, in theory, vested with a segment of imperial authority commensurate with his position in the hierarchy. In their training and indoctrination, officials were not encouraged to think of themselves as public servants.

The coming of democracy has changed the situation somewhat in recent years. The Constitution proclaims that "All public officials are servants of the whole community and not any group thereof." Although government agencies are aware of the need to maintain good public relations, the notion that the bureaucrat is a "public servant" is as yet somewhat alien to the Japanese mentality. When an individual becomes an official, he has, according to the prevailing scale of values, achieved status and prestige, and he tends to show it. By the same token,

[8] Hideo Shimizu, "Tokyo Daigaku Hogakubu" [Faculty of Law, Tokyo University], *Tembo,* No. 76 (April 1965), 110–29.

the expectation which seems to prevail among the general public is that bureaucrats are an arrogant and haughty lot. Although there is a good deal of grumbling about the way in which officials tend to treat the public, the average citizen finds it more expedient to bow low and assume a humble air when approaching officials.

Status Consciousness. The strong sense of hierarchy that prevails throughout Japanese society is naturally also manifested in the bureaucracy. In what is still one of the most interesting accounts of the bureaucracy, Kazuo Imai, a former bureaucrat, discusses the importance of status considerations.[9] According to him, higher officials ordinarily got tables with a green tablecloth, a swivel chair, and a telephone. A lower-ranking official who aspired to higher rank once brought a green tablecloth from home; it became the subject of much discussion in the office, and his superiors finally made him get rid of it. Again, a bureau chief was given a separate office, four bookshelves and ten chairs for guests; a section chief got, in addition to a table with a green tablecloth, two bookshelves and three to five chairs for guests; lower civil servants got no chairs for guests. The sense of hierarchy was even carried over into private life. An official was once transferred because his child, who was in the same class as his superior's child, got better grades.

Imai also states that promotions were based to a large extent on personal connections, and on the year of graduation from college. Kubota's study seems to substantiate the latter point. He found that no higher officials got demoted, and that promotions came most rapidly for graduates of the law faculty of Tokyo University and "in closest conformity with seniority."[10] Under the National Public Service Law, which is administered by the National Personnel Authority established in 1948, positions should be classified according to duties and responsibilities; employees are to be appointed and promoted on the basis of examinations, meritorious performance, and demonstrated

[9] Kazuo Imai, *Kanryo, Sono Seitai to Naimaku* [Bureaucrats, Their Modes of Life and Behind-the-scenes Activities] (Tokyo: Yomiuri Shimbun-sha, 1953), pp. 57ff.
[10] Kubota, *op. cit.*, p. 131.

abilities. Marshall Dimock, in his book *The Japanese Technocracy*, comments: "As might be imagined, the system has not responded completely to these requirements, and the ideal civil service is not yet a reality in Japan."[11]

LEGALISM

The Japanese bureaucracy is highly legalistic in its approach to administrative problems. The average bureaucrat likes to have every official act authorized in advance by a specific regulation or statute. When confronted by a situation that calls for a decision, the official usually runs to the bookshelf where the regulations and manuals are kept and starts to thumb through the pages looking for a law or ordinance that would cover the particular case. If no statute can be found and if there are no precedents, which are a great arbiter of Japanese administrative practice, a decision is likely to be postponed. According to an American observer of Japanese administration, "The difficulty of securing decisions, a chronic plague of large organizations, severely afflicts the Japanese government."[12]

One might interpret this addiction to legalism as showing a preference for "government by law." But this course leads us to a paradox: Law and legal institutions are underdeveloped in Japanese society and culture, yet administrators prefer "government by law." One plausible explanation for this seeming paradox may be found in the character of Japanese social relations. Most Japanese feel comfortable when social interaction takes place on a highly personal basis; when a bureaucrat transacts official business with a friend or someone who has been introduced to him through mutual friends, he can behave according to the dictates of social custom. It is only when an administrator has to deal with a total stranger in an impersonal, formalized social situation that he seeks refuge in the "law." Resort to law in the Japanese context, therefore, is not the

[11] Marshall Dimock, *The Japanese Technocracy* (New York: Walker/Weatherhill, 1968), p. 108.

[12] Milton J. Esman, "Japanese Administration—A Comparative View," *Public Administration Review*, vol. 7 (Spring 1947), p. 105.

attainment of justice, but a retreat from a difficult social situation.

FRAGMENTATION

When the Occupation began to apply pressure for the reform of the administrative system, it found that the structure of the upper levels of the civil service had first of all to be clarified. "Surprising though it may seem to one accustomed to the American practice of charting organizations and work operations, the Japanese had not, prior to the Occupation, attempted to chart their vast and complex organizations of government." In order to create such a picture of the functional interrelationships of ministries and administrative agencies to each other, to the prime minister and cabinet, and to the legislature and the judiciary, the staff was "faced with the problem of digging necessary data out of unindexed official documents, and facts from officials whose concepts of organization were often vague."[13]

Accounts by people who have held posts in the Japanese government are pretty much in agreement that the government structure is terribly fragmented. Each section, each bureau, and each ministry is highly jealous of its prerogatives, and there is relatively little coordination of activities. Pertinent documents, which are often vital if intelligent decisions are to be made, are kept by individual officials who often refuse to show them to other administrators. On this point, Imai relates his personal experiences:

> Shortly after I assumed my position in the government service, I was sent to the next section to borrow some documentary materials. As I recall it, they had to do with statistics which had been collected from every prefecture in the country. It seemed that the next section no longer had much need for these documents, since the study it had been making based on them was now completed; but they put up a lot

[13] Supreme Commander for the Allied Powers, *Political Reorientation of Japan* (Washington, D.C.: Government Printing Office, 1949), Vol. 1, p. 256.

of arguments and refused to lend them to me. I still remember the parting words of the man in charge of the section with whom I had negotiated, since they were out of this world. He said, "If this data is so essential, why doesn't your section send letters to the prefectures and get them?"[14]

The problem of separatist tendencies also exists at the interministry level. Dimock comments that "There is hardly a country in the world today where top-level coordination of government, if not the chief administrative problem, runs a close second. Japan is no exception."[15] Problems which necessitate a number of ministries and agencies working together are sometimes almost impossible to solve because bureaucracies have vested interests they want to defend. Bureaucratic fragmentation is perhaps aggravated in the Japanese case by certain structural features. For instance, there is a standing committee in the Diet for each ministry, and close working relations have naturally developed between the committees and the ministries. Moreover, the ruling Liberal Democratic party also has standing committees that parallel the ministries. The result is a situation in which the "individual influences on the ministries are stronger than the influence of the party as a whole upon the legislative and executive branches as a whole."[16] Japanese authorities are fully aware of the problem, and several commissions charged with recommending administrative reforms have tried to cope with it over the years. As these commissions have found, it is one thing to make recommendations, but quite another to get them adopted.

DECISION-MAKING STYLE

The conventional charts on Japanese governmental organization show a series of boxes arranged vertically and connected with solid or dotted lines indicating the flow of authority. The lines point downward, suggesting that the upper levels issue

[14] Imai, *op. cit.*, p. 142. Translation by the author.
[15] Dimock, *op. cit.*, p. 130.
[16] *Ibid.*, p. 133.

orders which are then carried out by the lower levels. This may be true insofar as the structure of formal authority goes, but in practice it is often different. It has been said that in a Japanese government office, "the superiors do not use their inferiors, but rather the inferiors use their supporters."[17]

The reason for this is the style of decision making that obtains in many organizations in Japan. The person at the head of an organization seldom makes a decision that then binds his subordinates to a particular course of action. Rather, the important thing is the group—the hamlet, the business firm, the labor union, the government agency, and at the most comprehensive level, the Japanese nation—and its growth and prosperity. This is best achieved when the group has unity, cohesion, and harmony, which in turn call for a constant flow of communication within the group and the presence of a leader or leaders who can articulate its goals, moods, and learnings. "The function of a Japanese leader," according to one observer, "is to anticipate (in the sense of feeling according to a deep communion with all his associates) the expression of a desire (or an opinion or action) which is so essentially experienced by everybody concerned that unanimity of agreement is already assured before a proposal is made."[18] When the group has reached a point where it is, so to speak, ripe for a decision, someone in the group who is well informed on the matter will draw up a proposal that will be circulated through the organization and formally approved by individuals who affix their seals to the document. The Japanese term for this document is *ringisho*, and this particular system is known as *ringisei* (*ringi*, "to ask from below").

According to Tsuji, a well-known authority on Japanese public administration, various commissions studying administrative reform have recommended modification of the practice of circulating documents. One commission in 1964 recommended the adoption of an allocation system, whereby "higher civil servants would assign tasks to qualified subordinate administrators and

[17] Imai, *op. cit.*, p. 104.
[18] Robert Ballon (ed.), *Doing Business in Japan* (Tokyo: Sophia University–Tuttle, 1967), p. 32.

would be responsible for checking their results, thus bringing about a feedback effect in Japanese public administration."[19] Tsuji's view is that the problem lies in the lack of staff services. "If higher executives are really to lead, able and experienced staff members to help them are indispensable."[20]

THE BUREAUCRACY AND INTEREST GROUPS

As we stated earlier, bureaucracy is particularly concerned with the output side of the political system. Government agencies are in a position to affect the welfare of individuals, business firms, organizations, and local communities through their power to grant licenses, to provide subsidies, and to purchase goods and services. Ishida has argued that whereas the stronger pressure groups work through party leaders, the weaker ones rely heavily on the bureaucracy: "Many of these groups look to the bureaucracy to help them strengthen their organizational foundations through government legislation legalizing their status and providing for compulsory membership."[21] In dealing with officials, personal contacts are understandably helpful. One of the most important functions of legislators at both the national and prefectural levels is to intercede with officials on behalf of their constituents. In his study of prefectural assemblies, Kim found that assemblymen are aware of interest groups and "feel they ought to render assistance as requested in facilitating a group's access to the administration officials."[22]

Corporations sometimes find it useful to put retired bureaucrats on the payroll. Although there is no prescribed retirement age in the Japanese civil service, by custom officials are ex-

[19] Kiyoaki Tsuji, "Decision-making in the Japanese Government: A Study of *Ringisei*," in Robert E. Ward (ed.), *Political Development in Modern Japan* (Princeton, N.J.: Princeton University Press, 1968), p. 471.

[20] *Ibid*., p. 472.

[21] Takeshi Ishida, "Pressure Groups in Japan," *Journal of Social and Political Ideas in Japan,* 2, 3 (December 1964), 109.

[22] Young C. Kim, "Role Orientations and Behavior: The Case of Japanese Prefectural Assemblymen in Chiba and Kanagawa," *The Western Political Quarterly,* 22, 2 (June 1969), 397.

pected to retire in their late forties and early fifties, so they naturally cultivate contacts for work to occupy the many productive years they will have after they leave government. Kubota has found that about 60 percent of the higher civil servants in his sample obtained employment after retirement from government service in public corporations and in private business firms.[23] As might be expected, he found a large number from the Ministry of International Trade and Industry and from the Economic Stabilization Board entering business; many from the Transportation Ministry going to work for railroads, bus lines, and shipping companies; and those from Telecommunications and Postal Services finding positions in private communications and transportation companies.

A more permanent and institutionalized connection between a ministry and its clientele is established through organizations known as *gaikaku dantai*, or "external organizations." These are semi-official organizations funded by the government to maintain liaison between the agency and the public. They may undertake research, publish booklets and journals, and engage in public relations activities. Many of their officers are retired bureaucrats or even officials who still retain posts in the government. Another important function of these external organizations, which number in the hundreds, is to serve as steppingstones to elective office. When a bureaucrat decides to resign from the civil service and run for elective office, he often seeks the support of these organizations, with which he has had close contact while serving as an administrator.

23 Kubota, *op. cit.*, p. 155.

8 Political Parties

It is somewhat difficult to characterize the Japanese party system. Some people have called it a "one-and-a-half party system," because the chief opposition party has never been able to come to power, although it does function to prevent monolithic one-party rule. But the one-and-a-half label is also misleading in the sense that there are actually multiple parties—five, to be exact. Again, however, it is not a multiparty system in the precise meaning of the term, because one party consistently controls the government without having to share power in a coalition arrangement. Perhaps the clearest way to describe the Japanese situation is to call it a one-party-dominant system. Such a system, of course, is not unique to Japan: In Mexico, the Partido Revolucionario Institucional (PRI) dominates the government election after election, as does the Congress Party at the national level in India.

THE HISTORICAL DEVELOPMENT OF PARTIES

The origins of political parties go back to the nineteenth century. The first parties were organized in the 1870s, and from these beginnings there evolved by the 1920s two so-called bourgeois parties—the Society of Political Friends (Seiyukai) and the Popular Rule Party (Minseito). The former appealed somewhat more to the rural and agrarian elements, while the latter was more urban and probusiness in its outlook. With the granting of universal manhood suffrage in 1925, the way was paved for the emergence of left-wing parties based in varying degrees on Marxist principles.

Japan's industrialization, which gave rise to a small urban working class, presented certain political difficulties, because those in power feared that a militant working-class movement allied with the left-wing might tear the social fabric apart. The government discouraged the growth of labor unions, periodically suppressed the early socialist movement, and banned the Communist Party formed in 1921. Nevertheless, so-called proletarian parties ran candidates in the 1928 election (the first since the universal manhood suffrage law) and in subsequent elections, but were never able to make much headway. This was in part because of a hostile atmosphere that worsened after the invasion of Manchuria in 1931, when a wave of intense nationalism swept the country. Even liberals were harassed. Academics who were critical of the government were sometimes fired from their jobs, publications were censored for "dangerous thoughts," and Communist activists were jailed or forced into exile. Memories of this period are still vivid among those who belong to the Left, and the fear of a possible revival of political repression reminiscent of the 1930s, more than any other single issue, serves to divide the opposition from the ruling conservative party.

In 1940 even the so-called bourgeois parties were compelled to dissolve; they were replaced by the Imperial Rule Assistance Association, a government-sponsored body which was to be the sole organ of political expression. Informal and personal groupings of politicians, however, continued to exist, and these groupings provided the nucleus of the new parties formed soon after the end of World War II in 1945. It was characteristic of the disorganized state of affairs that in the beginning, hundreds of political clubs, societies, and so-called parties were founded.

Before long, four principal parties emerged. The Liberal party (Jiyuto) and the Progressive party (Shimpoto) were both conservative and traced their roots in a very general way to the prewar Seiyukai and Minseito, respectively. The Socialist party (Nihon Shakaito) was made up of men who had been active in the prewar proletarian parties. Being composed of socialists of varying political hues, the Socialist party has been plagued by internal bickering and factionalism. The Japanese Communist Party (Nihon Kyosanto), acquiring legal status for the first time, came to be led by Communists who had either been released from jail or returned from exile in Russia or Communist China.

For about a decade after the end of the war, the party lineup remained rather fluid. On the socialist side, the party split into right and left wings, but managed to reunite in 1955, only to break up into the Socialist party and a right-wing splinter group, the Democratic Socialist party, in 1959. On the conservative side, the Progressive party went through a series of reorganizations, but it finally united with the Liberal party in 1955 to form the present Liberal Democratic party.

PARTY STRUCTURE

The Conservative and Socialist Parties. In Japan, as in other countries, interested citizens are free to join political parties of their choice. Except for the Communist Party, which looks into the ideological orientation of prospective members, parties do not maintain rigid entrance requirements. Actually, however, relatively few people go to the trouble of joining a party, paying dues regularly, and taking part in its activities. The core of Japanese parties therefore consists of professional politicians, especially members of the National Diet.

All parties have some kind of machinery to keep things running, and structurally there are no substantial differences between the conservative and socialist parties. The parties maintain a headquarters organization in Tokyo with branches in the prefectures and cities and towns. In theory, the party convention, usually held annually, determines party policies and chooses the more important officers. In the case of the Liberal Democratic party, the president is elected by a secret ballot for a term of two years at a party conference attended by all Diet members belonging to the party and by one delegate from each of the prefectural federations of local branches. If no candidate secures a majority vote on the first ballot, the two highest vote-getters compete in a second-round election. Since the Liberal

Democratic party is the ruling party, its president will be the prime minister. He is assisted by a small number of key party leaders. The secretary-general has the responsibility of keeping the party machinery running smoothly. In addition, the chairmen of two important committees, the Policy Research Committee and the Executive Committee, exercise a great deal of power.

The Policy Research Committee is a large and complex body consisting of a chairman, no more than five vice-chairmen, a deliberation council, and fifteen permanent divisions, plus any number of special ad hoc committees.[1] All matters pertaining to party policy and all bills that are to be presented to the National Diet must first be approved by the Policy Research Committee and then passed on to the Executive Committee for its approval. Because it acts as a gatekeeper for proposed legislation, the Policy Research Committee is subjected to pressure from all kinds of interest groups and to a proliferation of subcommittees.

The Executive Committee is the highest decision-making body within the party. It oversees the work of all party committees, and it must approve all bills that are to be presented to the legislature. In practice, the Executive Committee acts as a kind of appeals body to the Policy Research Committee. Pressure groups that have been turned down by the former body can and do bring their case before the Executive Committee. Its membership is drawn from members of the House of Councillors and the House of Representatives, and those appointed by the party president. In practice, representatives of all party factions will be placed on the Executive Committee.

Since the Socialists are not a ruling party, their party machinery need not be so elaborate. There is no party president; the corresponding position is that of chairman of the Central Executive Committee. The other party leader is the secretary-general. Like the Liberal Democratic party, its core is made up of Socialist Diet members; it was not until recently that non-Diet members were permitted to become members of the Central Executive Committee.

[1] Haruhiro Fukui, *Party in Power: The Japanese Liberal-Democrats and Policy-making* (Berkeley, Calif.: University of California Press, 1970), p. 83.

Over the years, relatively few people have held the posts of chairman of the Central Executive Committee and secretary-general. Until recently, one qualification was a record of activity in the prewar left-wing movement, but of course this will change as the party makes the transition to postwar leaders. Generally, if one of the two top posts goes to a leader from one faction within the party, the other position is given to someone representing another faction.

The National Convention of the Socialist party is supposed to be the top decision-making body. Both the plenary sessions and the committee meetings can sometimes be boisterous affairs. But as some observers note, "as in virtually all parties, the convention is a very imperfect instrument for either generating policies or holding leadership accountable for past performance."[2]

Neither the Liberal Democrats nor the Socialists have much in the way of local organization. Both parties have branches, which in turn are organized into prefectural federations. Although the Socialists claim to be the party that represents the interests of the masses, it cannot be considered a mass organization by any stretch of the imagination. Socialist leaders are aware of this weakness and engage in verbal self-flagellation about the lack of grass roots organization, but they have not been able to remedy the situation. In terms of party organization at the local level, the conservatives are no better off; but they have the advantage of being able to enlist the support of all kinds of nonparty groups—the PTA, cooperatives, and the like. Moreover, a great many local officials, mayors, city councilmen, and governors are conservative party supporters, even though they may run for office as independents.

Minor Parties. The Democratic Socialist party is a splinter group of right-wing socialists who split off from the main party in 1959. Not surprisingly, its organizational structure is much like that of the parent body. It holds a national convention every year, but policy is really controlled by the Central Executive Committee. Strictly speaking, the Democratic Socialist party

[2] Allan B. Cole, George O. Totten, and Cecil H. Uyehara, *Socialist Parties in Postwar Japan* (New Haven, Conn.: Yale University Press, 1966), p. 250.

cannot be considered a national party, since it does not run candidates in all electoral districts.

The structure of the Japan Communist Party is similar to that of Communist parties elsewhere. Theoretically, the Party Congress is all-powerful, but in fact power is lodged in the Presidium, and particularly in its Executive Committee. In addition, there is a Party Secretariat and a Central Committee with a little more than sixty regular members and more than forty alternates. The party is run on the basis of democratic centralism. Like most Communist parties in the Third World, the Japanese Party has been affected by the Sino-Soviet split. In the mid-1960s two small splinter groups broke off, one taking a pro-Soviet position; the other, a Pro-Peking stance. The main body, however, adopted a more neutralist position vis-à-vis the Sino-Soviet controversy, and stressed its independence from the two main Communist power centers and a less revolutionary policy in domestic politics. Both policy positions appear to have paid off in the form of increased appeal to the voters.

The fifth and newest party, the Clean Government party (Komeito), which is the political arm of a Buddhist religious organization, the Soka Gakkai (Value Creation Society), was formed in 1964. Its guiding body is the Central Executive Committee, and the lines of authority go downward through the Secretariat, the Organization Bureau, local headquarters, the prefectural federations, and the branches at the bottom of the pyramid. The Komeito has the advantage of being able to utilize the strong organizational structure of its parent body. The Soka Gakkai is organized at the grass roots level into what might be called squads, each with a leader. These small face-to-face groups meet regularly to worship together and to help each other out, and thus represent rather cohesive groups easily mobilized for political purposes. Thanks to this kind of organization, the Komeito has experienced remarkable growth.

PARTY LEADERSHIP

Factions. The Liberal Democratic party—and even the Socialist party—may be thought of as basically federations of factions. The faction consists of a leader—that is, a politician—with a certain number of followers, usually somewhere between twenty and fifty. The number is important: If a leader has too few followers, he is weak; but if he has too many, he may not be able to provide the material and other benefits he must give to his followers in return for loyal support. There is a kind of patron-client relationship here. Once formed, these factions acquire stability and last until the leader retires or dies, at which point the faction might be transferred to one of his lieutenants, although when that happens some of the followers may be enticed to join other factions. The faction generally acquires the name of its leader.

Watanabe, a well-informed student of factions, cites four reasons for their existence.[3] First, before the war, the few large zaibatsu firms gave the parties lump sums, but today there are many firms giving money, so that political leaders who have access to these funds can support a certain number of followers. Second, the form of electoral competition (about which more will be said in the next chapter) pits politicians in the same party against each other, and these politicians end up in different factions. Third, Diet members who seek to become cabinet members can do so only through membership in factions. In order to become president of the Liberal Democratic party and hence prime minister, a leader must build a winning coalition by promising cabinet positions as rewards. Within the faction, there is a rank order in which members are entitled to cabinet appointments. The order is determined by such factors as the number of times a man has been elected, his career background, and the tangible and intangible benefits he has brought to the faction leader. Fourth, Watanabe cites certain historical factors: resentment of the dictatorial rule exercised by Prime Minister Yoshida in the 1950s; the dispersion of leadership among a number of lesser politicians after the retirement of Yoshida and Hatoyama; and the conservative merger in 1955 without prior agreement on ideological issues and policy preferences among those entering into it.

One interesting problem for political scientists has to do

[3] Tsuneo Watanabe, *Toshu to Seito* [Party Leaders and Political Parties] (Tokyo: Kobundo, 1961), pp. 96–98.

with the qualifications that enable a politician to become a faction leader. Neither personality type nor career background appear to be involved. Some faction leaders have been ex-civil servants, others have been journalists, and still others, businessmen. Moreover, ideological position does not seem to be particularly important, which means that a faction does not represent a commitment to a political program or a set of issues. In short, personal considerations—the desire on the part of an ambitious politician to become one of the party leaders, plus the wish on the part of followers to share in money and offices—enter into the forming and sustaining of factions.

The existence of factions is often decried by journalists and other observers; even professional politicians have urged their abolition from time to time, but to no avail. Granted that factionalism has some pernicious effects—for example, it impedes intraparty democracy and unity—its consequences are not entirely negative. Fukui has suggested that factions facilitate intraparty communication: "Whereas a meeting of four hundred members would no doubt make it rather difficult for each to express his views freely and for all to come to agreement on specific problems, a relatively small group of a few dozen members may find it much easier to satisfy such needs."[4] Perhaps more important, it leads to a more pluralistic form of politics. The existence of factions tempers the authority of the prime minister and permits different points of view to be held and expressed within the party. As Baerwald says, "Factions may not be the most obvious device for rational government, and their reasons for supporting one or another individual for a high post or this or that policy alternative may be based upon a desire for power rather than for 'what is good for Japan' (a favorite theme of the senior bureaucrats), but without them Japanese politics would be far less open than it is."[5]

The Leaders. Since the primary purpose of all political parties (except perhaps the Communist Party) is to get their leaders

[4] Fukui, *op. cit.*, p. 137.
[5] Hans H. Baerwald, "Tento-Mura: At the Making of a Cabinet," in Lucian W. Pye (ed.), *Cases in Comparative Politics: Asia* (Boston: Little, Brown, 1970), p. 83.

into office and since the largest single block of elective posts is found in the National Diet, it is natural that Diet members should carry great weight in party affairs. Nowadays, most party leaders are members of the House of Representatives.

One of the striking characteristics of these leaders is that although they hold elective office, they are singularly lacking in charismatic qualities. We have already mentioned that Japan has never produced a Churchill, a de Gaulle, or a Kennedy, a man with magnetism and great popular appeal. Rather, the typical Japanese political leader is a person with good connections for raising funds, skilled in behind-the-scenes political maneuvering, and loyal to his superiors and benevolent to his followers. One of the reasons for this must certainly be the existence of factionalism. Scalapino and Masumi have spoken of the "paradox of Japan's being an open society made up of closed components."[6] The party structure is closed to the loner, the politician unaffiliated with some faction. To get anywhere a man must join a faction, which means he must wait until he achieves a prominent position within his faction through seniority. If the personal relationships within a party were more fluid and if there were, as a consequence, more loners, a newcomer would have a chance to rise to the top quickly. The existence of the faction structure tends to impede the development of new and, more important, novel types of leadership. One of the consequences is that compelling problems are unlikely to be solved through bold, innovative, and venturesome political leadership. In this sense Japan is rather different from Great Britain, which, as Dimock has pointed out, handles crisis situations superbly. In Japan, the "prominent features are rationality, system, bureaucracy, and consensus, as well as a few risktakers outside this formal system."[7]

A look at political leadership also tells us something about basic change in Japanese politics. If we assume that political upheavals are registered in the makeup of the political elite, we

[6] Robert A. Scalapino and Junnosuke Masumi, *Parties and Politics in Contemporary Japan* (Berkeley, Calif.: University of California Press, 1962), p. 153.

[7] Marshall Dimock, *The Japanese Technocracy* (New York: Walker/Weatherhill, 1968), p. 37.

can get some idea of the essential continuity in Japanese political life despite war, defeat, and the Occupation. One of the striking features of party leadership, among both conservatives and the left-wing, is the relatively large number of men who are carryovers from the prewar period. We are now, however, entering a period of transition, and with every passing year those who had established themselves in the system prior to the war will drop out through retirement and death, and will be replaced by individuals who got their start after 1945. It will be interesting to see the extent to which "second generation" leaders—that is, sons of political leaders who are in a position to capitalize on their father's name and following—will be able to get a foothold in politics. (About 150 representatives elected in the 1967 election are said to be sons of politicians.) This brings us to the subject of how party leaders are brought into the system.

LEADERSHIP RECRUITMENT

For the Liberal Democratic party, there are four major roads to party positions.

The Bureaucracy. Before the war, when parties were weak and unable to control the government, career civil servants were often named to cabinet positions. Under the new Constitution, a change was made in the rules of the game; the majority of cabinet members must now be drawn from the National Diet. Ambitious bureaucrats who wish to get to the top must leave the bureaucracy, run for elective office, and attain leadership positions within the party.

Fortunately for them, civil servants are in a good position to take these steps. While in the bureaucracy they can take advantage of their office to cultivate contacts with corporations, interest groups, local political leaders and others who will be able to help them once they launch themselves in a new political career. Moreover, voters are generally impressed by anyone whose credentials include long civil service employment, and the amount of inherent vote-getting power they enjoy is not lost on party leaders. When they retire from the civil service, they do not have too much difficulty getting party endorsement in running for the House of Councillors or the House of Representatives. If elected, they rise fairly rapidly to positions of leadership within the conservative party because of their knowledge and administrative skills and their connections with government agencies.

According to Fukui's calculations, between 1958 and 1967 the percentage of ex-bureaucrats elected to the House of Representatives has varied slightly between 23.4 and 26.0 percent, that is, roughly 1 out of 4. The proportion of ex-bureaucrats appointed to cabinet positions is somewhat higher, and has ranged between one-third to one-half during the same time span. Thus, they are somewhat overrepresented at the cabinet level. They are also strong in the decision-making machinery within the party. Fukui's conclusion is that bureaucrats "are almost invariably associated with the nuclear group of party decision-makers thanks to their training and experience, which are particularly relevant to the legislative functions and responsibilities of a ministerial party under the present cabinet system."[8]

Local Politics. One of the effects of constitutional reform was an increase in the number of elective offices at the subnational level. In theory, therefore, the possibility of entry into national politics via the local route should have been markedly enhanced. The empirical evidence, however, does not appear to substantiate this hypothesis. Fukui, who has studied this phenomenon back as far as 1890, has shown how there has been a steady decrease in the proportion of members of the House of Representatives with a background in local politics. From 1890 to 1904, local politicians accounted for almost three-fourths of the Diet members; in 1936, they were about one-half; in the 1955 to 1965 period, they were just over one-fourth.[9]

A striking difference between the ex-bureaucrats in the Diet and their fellow-members with local backgrounds is level of

[8] Fukui, *op. cit.*, pp. 68–69.
[9] *Ibid.*, Appendix 1, pp. 271–73.

education. Almost 90 percent of the former were graduated from Tokyo University, while only 6.5 percent of the latter were Tokyo University alumni (in 1965). Quite obviously, local politics does not appeal to the Tokyo University graduate; he prefers a bureaucratic career either in government or in corporations. On the other hand, some of the graduates of private colleges as well as those who did not go to college at all are trying their hand at local politics since bureaucratic careers are closed to them. This route can and does lead to national politics, but the going is difficult, partly because salaries in local and prefectural government agencies are low.

Business. Since the mid-1950s, roughly one-fifth of the Liberal Democratic members of the House of Representatives may be classified as businessmen. Although there appears to be no up-to-date statistical data on this point, the impression one gets is that most of the businessmen in the Diet are drawn from small and medium-sized businesses and perhaps from the middle range of big business. No businessman or corporation executive has held the post of prime minister since 1945, but it is conceivable that at some future date a businessman might attain that position and thus set a precedent. Among the dozen or so factions within the Liberal Democratic party in recent years, at least three were led by businessmen. There is no doubt that those who can draw income from their business enterprises have an advantage in that it generally takes money to win an election; and once in office, entertainment costs and other outlays can easily exceed the salary received. As business enterprises and businessmen become more important in the scheme of things, those involved in business are likely to assume more prominence in politics. They are already in a sense within the system, for many of them are related to politicians through marriage and form one part of the tightly knit Japanese elite.

The Professions. In many Western countries, lawyers are overrepresented in legislative halls. Because Japanese culture does not encourage litigation, the legal profession in Japan is amazingly small. Still, lawyers do represent one of the more noticeable professional groups in the House of Representatives. Historically, lawyers have comprised as much as one-fifth of the membership, but since the conservative merger in 1955, their representation has declined sharply. It is difficult to say whether this is a temporary phenomenon, for it would appear that lawyers and law-making form a natural combination. Moreover, lawyers are in the happy position of being able to maintain a law office while holding a post in the Diet.

The most serious competitors to lawyers are journalists. Tanzan Ishibashi, president and editor-in-chief of a well-known economics magazine, *Toyo Keizai (Oriental Economist)*, became prime minister late in 1956. (He served only a short term because of illness.) Journalism and writing do enable individuals to become well known, and some are able to capitalize on this to get into politics. The spread of television has also provided opportunities for well-known entertainers to enter politics. A few have achieved spectacular victories, especially in recent House of Councillors elections. As in the United States, the mass media represent an important element in the political life of the nation.

The Socialists also recruit leaders through these channels, but their overall pattern is of course somewhat different. Labor union officials make up more than half the Socialist members of the two houses in the National Diet, which tells us something of the close tie between organized labor and the Socialist party. The second largest group is made up of local politicians, who account for 1 out of 5 members. Civil servants, businessmen, and journalists combined represent only about one-tenth of the Socialist delegation to the national legislature.

THE SOCIAL BASE OF PARTIES

If parties are to enjoy stability and continuity, they must have some meaningful relationship to social classes and groups; otherwise, they are nothing more than coteries of individuals who come together and separate in a fluid fashion. As we have suggested, the personal element looms large in Japanese parties; yet it would be a mistake to conclude that Japanese parties are completely divorced from social groupings.

There now exists a considerable body of data drawn from public opinion surveys and studies of voter attitudes that gives us some idea of the social base of Japanese political parties. Briefly stated, this seems to be the situation:

1. The Liberal Democratic party is a national party in that it draws support from all sections of the country and from all social classes. But it is quite clear that its strongest appeal is to what we might call the entrepreneurial classes. Not only do the large corporations back the party, but so do managerial personnel as well as medium- and small-scale businessmen. The farmers are the other chief basis of support.

2. The Socialist party is the party of organized labor and in particular of those unions affiliated with the General Council of Trade Unions (Sohyo). Probably at least one-third or more of white collar as well as blue collar workers in large-scale enterprises, especially government corporations, support the Socialist party.

3. The Democratic Socialists also appeal to organized labor, but to those unions affiliated with the Japanese Confederation of Labor (Domei), which is much smaller than Sohyo.

The Clean Government party is strong in the metropolitan areas and appeals mostly to the lower economic classes, particularly to men and women who have recently migrated from the rural areas. These individuals are often beset by feelings of insecurity and rootlessness and manage to get integrated into urban life and into politics through the Soka Gakkai organization. In short, the party appeals to those classes neglected by the other parties.

Like the Clean Government party, the Communist Party is also a metropolitan party, but it appeals to a different group of people. The Communist organization extends into factories and includes workers, as one might expect; but it also appeals to the better educated, and it includes among its supporters university students, writers, and intellectuals.

Thus, in a broad way Japanese parties do represent different economic interests, educational levels, and social values and help to account for their persistence. In the long run, however, party stability depends on the transmission of loyalty to the party across generations—that is, on political socialization. As yet, political socialization is a subject that has been little studied in Japan. Research findings based on relatively limited samples are somewhat contradictory. The most recent one by Kubota and Ward[10] found a "moderate" degree of correspondence in party identification between parents and their children. Their data also suggest that the Communist families in their sample did the best job of transmitting party loyalty to the younger generation, followed by the Liberal Democratic and Clean Government parties.

Kubota and Ward found, moreover, that urban families and those in which the father was a member of a labor union were most effective in transmitting party identification. These findings are suggestive but by no means conclusive. Until more research has been done on political socialization in Japan, we cannot make judgments with any degree of confidence. One thing, however, does seem fairly certain. Partisanship gains stability with the passage of time. Converse has noted that there is a progressive "binding in" of popular loyalties to one or another of the competing political parties. He argues further that the maturity of a party system is approached after about two-and-a-half generations.[11] When measured against such a standard, the Japanese party system is still young and, by implication, not particularly stable.

[10] Akira Kubota and Robert E. Ward, "Family Influence in Political Socialization in Japan," *Comparative Political Studies*, 3, 2 (July 1970), 140–75.

[11] Philip E. Converse, "Of Time and Partisan Stability," *Comparative Political Studies*, 2, 2 (July 1969), 138–71.

9 The Electorate and Electoral Behavior

In the previous chapter, we touched on the social basis of parties; parties and voters, after all, are interrelated. On the one hand, parties articulate cleavages, strains, and conflicting interests in the social structure; on the other hand, they also compel citizens to make alliances across cleavage lines and to make choices among policy preferences.

Because parties articulate cleavages, the historical milieu in which they develop greatly affects their character. The integrative function of parties (getting people of diverse views to work together), which is important in a democracy, is rendered difficult and perhaps impossible if the social cleavages rest on what people feel are fundamental differences. Most if not all the strains and cleavages in modernized countries can be traced to the two revolutions that have occurred: the national revolution and the industrial revolution. The former was concerned with nation-building—the creation of a national culture and the resistance to it on the part of linguistic, ethnic, and religious groups. The latter gave rise to conflicts between landed interests and industrial entrepreneurs, and between capitalists and workers.[1] Fortunately for Japan, nation-building took place over a relatively long span of time and without great conflict between linguistic, ethnic, or religious groups. The industrial revolution did, however, pose problems of how increasing numbers of workers and agricultural tenants owning little or no property

[1] Seymour M. Lipset and Stein Rokkan (eds.), *Party Systems and Voter Alignments* (New York: Free Press, 1967), p. 14.

should be incorporated into the political system. One way to approach this problem is to look at the expansion of the electorate.

EXPANSION OF THE ELECTORATE

The first election law, adopted in 1889, governed the election of members of the House of Representatives and rested on the principle of a highly restricted electorate. The ballot was limited to men 25 years of age and over who paid 15 yen in direct national taxes, in the form of either a land tax or an income tax. A further qualification was made in the provision that the land tax should be paid for a period of at least one year, and income taxes for at least three years. Finally, the voter was required to have resided in the electoral district for a year or more. A practical consequence of these restrictions was to limit the electorate to the larger landowners, a few businessmen, and high officials, and to exclude intellectuals and a large section of the urban population.

It was not long before the socialists began to agitate for a radical expansion of the electorate. The Manifesto of the short-lived Social Democratic party organized in 1901 argued that the party could achieve its aims once it gained a majority in the Diet, then, in its view, an organ of the "landlords and capitalists." "Once the right to vote passes into the hands of the majority of the people, the most important obstacle to attaining the interest of the majority will be overcome."[2] The following year, the League for Universal Manhood Suffrage (Futsu Senkyo Domei Kai) was formed under socialist auspices.

In 1900 the tax qualification was reduced from 15 to 10 yen, thereby increasing the number of men with the right to vote from 453,474 to 501,459. It is doubtful that this step had anything to do with agitation from the Left; rather, its motivation lay in more practical considerations. In the beginning the suffrage had been limited to landowners and other taxpayers on

[2] *Shakai Minshuto no sengen*, reprinted in Sakuzo Yoshino (ed.), *Meiji Bunka Zenshu*, 21 (Tokyo: Nihon Hyoron-sha, 1929), 536.

the theory that they were the pillars of conservatism and hence would not upset the political status quo. But the domination of the landed interests in the legislature also had its disadvantage, in the sense that the Diet was relatively unsympathetic to legislation intended to stimulate industrial development, especially when such development might take place at the expense of agriculture. The expansion of the electorate in 1900, therefore, came largely as a result of pressure from the urban districts and from commercial and industrial interests.

Three years later, in 1903, a bill calling for universal manhood suffrage was introduced in the Diet, but failed to pass. Another bill was approved by the lower house in 1911, but this was rejected by the House of Peers. During the debate in the House of Peers, a spokesman for the government argued against the bill in the following terms:

> The government wishes to indicate that it is absolutely opposed to the present bill. . . . The ideal of universal suffrage grew out of the theory of natural rights which was in vogue in Europe at one time. I believe that it is based on the very faulty and dangerous view that all people are born with the right to vote. At the present time this theory no longer has influence, and it goes without saying that people are not born with such rights. It is a gift which the state bestows. . . . If such a system is adopted, the knowledge [possessed by] the voters may decline, but it will never rise, and so I believe that it will have unfavorable results in selecting representatives of the people. We fear that in the end the majority of lower class people will override the minority of upper class people, and hence the government is absolutely opposed to this bill.[3]

The next expansion of the electorate came in 1919, when the tax qualification was again reduced, this time from 10 to 3 yen, thereby giving the vote to small landowners. But the tax qualification, small as it was, served to exclude the urban proletariat and some intellectuals in urban areas. Despite the reduction, sentiment in favor of universal manhood suffrage remained strong, fanned by the worldwide spread of Wilsonian ideals.

[3] Quoted in Yasuzo Suzuki, *Nihon Seiji no Kijun* [The Basis of Japanese Politics] (Tokyo: Toyo Keizai Shimposha, 1941), pp. 175–76.

Although even Hara, the first commoner to become premier, remained hostile to the expansion of the electorate on the ground that such expansion would destroy the class system which was the basis of stability, the proponents of universal suffrage—intellectuals, the big city press, and the Left generally—eventually won after a spirited campaign. In 1925 the universal manhood suffrage act was passed; it took effect in the 1928 national elections. The next large extension of the electorate occurred after the war, when, as a result of Occupation pressure, women were granted the right to vote for the first time.

Today Japan enjoys universal suffrage; yet it is evident that neither the hopes of the early socialists nor the fears of the conservatives have materialized. But it is also true that a persistent conservative-radical cleavage continues to be reflected in the alignment of parties and in the way in which the electorate divides.

VOTING TRENDS

A remarkable feature of Japanese elections is the consistent way in which the electorate has divided in casting its vote for party candidates. The electorate has not given its overwhelming support to one party, only to abandon it in the next election in favor of another. Since 1945, candidates endorsed by the conservative party or parties have held the majority. In recent years, however, the percentage of the vote cast for conservative candidates has been declining. In the early and mid-1960s, the Socialist party vote remained stable, but then declined rather sharply in the 1969 election. In contrast to the declining fortunes of the two larger parties, the three minor parties, and particularly the Clean Government party and the Communist Party, gained popularity in the late 1960s. The voting trend is summarized in Table 6.

As Table 6 shows, the total vote for the Liberal Democrats has leveled off at between 22 and 23 million. The growth in the number of votes resulting from population increase has there-

Table 6: Voting for the House of Representatives (in millions)

Date of Election	Liberal Democratic	Socialist	Democratic Socialist	Clean Government	Communist
1947	16.1	7.2			1.0
1949	19.2	4.1			3.0
1952	23.4	7.5			.9
1953	22.7	9.2			.7
1955	24.3	10.8			.7
1958	23.0	13.1			1.0
1960	22.7	10.3	3.5		1.2
1963	22.4	11.9	3.0		1.6
1967	22.4	12.8	3.4	2.5	2.2
1969	22.3	10.0	3.6	5.1	3.2

fore gone to the opposition parties. Quite clearly, the party system is becoming increasingly fragmented.

In Japan, as elsewhere, not all eligible voters take the trouble to go to the polls. In some countries the voter must first take steps to get himself registered to become eligible to vote. The Japanese are reluctant to leave the initiative for registration up to the voter, so the government itself compiles lists of eligible voters on the basis of various records, such as residence information, ration lists, and so on. The rate of electoral participation has been in a downtrend since 1958, particularly among male voters, and it seems to coincide with rapid economic growth and urbanization. It is possible to identify in a general way the types of voters who are more likely to abstain in elections. First, voting is inversely related to urbanization. Rural voters consistently turn out in larger numbers (proportionately) than do city dwellers. This is similar to countries like France and is in contrast to countries like the United States, where the cities tend to have a higher turnout rate. Second, in terms of age groups, the middle groups—that is, those between thirty and fifty years of age—are more likely to vote than those in their twenties and sixties. These differentials affect party fortunes in different ways; they would appear mostly to help the conservatives and penalize the progressives.

There are doubtless a number of reasons that can be cited

to help explain why individuals fail to go to the polls on election day. One of these may be the negative view of parties and politicians that appears to be widespread. There are people who tend to think of politics as something quite alien to their daily lives. To many individuals, government is detached from the people; it exists far away and is supposed to be benevolent and paternalistic, fair, and impartial—in short, nonpartisan. Party government, however, is by its nature partisan, a fact which repels some people.

VOTER PREFERENCES

A common way to characterize party alignments is to place them on a left-right scale. We have already discussed the ruling Liberal Democratic party and the opposition parties as representing a conservative-radial cleavage. Without doubt, ideology is a factor that helps unify a party and distinguish it from other parties. The Liberal Democratic party, for example, believes in capitalism, the promotion of business enterprise, and friendship with the United States. By contrast, the Socialist party stands in opposition to capitalism and in favor of socialism, looks on the United States as the embodiment of imperialism, and argues for friendship with all countries, including the Communist ones.

It is not clear, however, that many party members (as distinguished from party leaders) have a clear understanding of ideology, if by that term we mean a set of beliefs about man and his relation to society that are internally consistent. Converse, on the basis of American survey data, has come to the conclusion that those who had a reasonably clear conception of ideology, what he calls the "ideologues" and "near ideologues," came to about 15 percent of the population.[4] An empirical study of British voters concludes: "It is clear that the theory that a voter chooses among parties on the basis of their distance from his own position along a left-right spectrum is

[4] Philip E. Converse, "The Nature of Belief Systems in Mass Publics," in David Apter (ed.), *Ideology and Discontent* (New York: Free Press, 1964).

very far from describing how the great bulk of British electors make their choice."[5] The only Japanese study that deals with this problem is that done by Miyake and his colleagues. Their findings, based on a limited sample of the Japanese electorate, interestingly enough are very similar to Converse's characterization of American voters.[6]

One inference to be drawn is that members of various parties overlap in terms of political preferences. In other words, the Liberal Democratic party contains some individuals who are closer to the socialists in their views, and the Socialist party has members who are essentially conservative. In a study carried out in Tokyo in 1964, the conclusion was that among Liberal Democratic supporters, some 30 percent had progressive views, while 28 percent of those who supported left-wing parties were conservative in their ideas.[7] Thus, the Liberal Democratic and the Socialist parties may be characterized as follows: When we look at the leadership strata, the Liberal Democratic party is far to the right and the Socialist party is far to the left, whereas when we look at the membership, there is no sharp division, but an overlap in the middle.

Another way to look at party alignment is to place parties along a traditional-modern continuum. One of the hallmarks of traditional values is the importance ascribed to the family and filial piety. The survey on national character carried out in 1968 included a question on important moral principles. Four choices were given, from which each respondent could pick two: Filial piety, returning favors done for you by others, stressing one's rights, and valuing freedom. If we take those who chose filial piety as an important value, and classify them according to the political party they support, we find that at the top of the list are those who favor the Clean Government party (72 percent), followed by the Liberal Democratic party (64 percent), Socialist

[5] David Butler and Donald Stokes, *Political Change in Britain* (New York: St. Martin's, 1969), p. 212.

[6] Ichiro Miyake *et al.*, *Kotonaru Reberu no Senkyo ni okeru Tohyo Kodo no Kenkyu* [Study of Voting Behavior in Elections at Various Levels] (Tokyo: Sobunsha, 1967), p. 766–73.

[7] "Sengo Nihon ni okeru Yoto to Yato no Rikigaku" [The Dynamics of Government and Opposition in Postwar Japan] *Chosa Geppo,* 144 (December 1967), 9.

(56 percent), Democratic Socialist (53 percent), and the Communist (34 percent) far down at the bottom.[8]

Another more conventional way of looking at political parties and their supporters is to sort them out on the basis of their political ideology, that is, along the Left-Right or Conservative-Radical continuum. Quite clearly, the Liberal Democratic party would fall on the conservative side, while the two Marxist parties—Socialist and Communist—would have to be placed on the radical end of the continuum. The more moderate Democratic Socialist party probably ought to be considered more conservative than radical. The Clean Government party is somewhat difficult to characterize in terms of ideology, since it is in some respects anti-Establishment, but basically it accepts the capitalistic system and so should be considered as belonging within the conservative camp. If we were to combine the traditional-modern dimension with the conservative-radical scale, we could offer the combination shown in Table 7.

Table 7: Ideology, Traditionalism, and Party Support

Ideology	Traditional	Modern
Conservative	Liberal Democratic Clean Government	Democratic Socialist
Radical	Socialist	Communist

The material in Table 7 suggests several things. First, the Liberal Democratic and Clean Government parties are rather similar in terms of membership. Second, the greatest cleavage is between the Liberal Democratic and Clean Government parties and the Communists. One might infer from the table that the two minor parties, Clean Government and Communist, both metropolitan-based, would not compete for votes, and this is borne out by empirical data. Third, the Liberal Democratic, Socialist, and Democratic Socialist parties share either common ideological outlooks or traditional values, which, in

[8] Tokeisuri Kenkyujo, Kokumin-sei no Kenkyu [Study of National Character] (Tokyo: Tokeisuri Kenkyujo 1968), p. 91.

turn, would imply that their memberships overlap and that these three parties could find grounds for mutual accommodation.

Our discussion so far has suggested that voter preferences are influenced to some extent by ideology as articulated by parties and by attachment or lack thereof to traditional values. What about the personal qualifications of candidates? Do voters like certain kinds of candidates better than others?

We can discern several subtypes of candidates. First, in rural areas where traditional values are still strong, there are a small number of local notables who are active in politics, who have helped the villagers in personal and other matters and through such efforts have established patron-client relationships with them, and who have political connections with politicians in the higher levels of government. When these notables run for local office, they will not need to campaign actively because many of the villagers will vote for them. Such notables are also in a good position to persuade their clients to vote for candidates they happen to be backing in prefectural and national elections.

Second, some voters are influenced by a candidate's achievements in his chosen profession—a civil servant who has risen to an important position in the bureaucracy, a businessman who has built up a prosperous business, or a professional man, say a doctor, who has built up a good practice. Such voters are clearly being influenced by the image the candidate projects.

Third, some voters show a preference for a candidate who is perceived to be in a position to bring benefits to the community or organization—for example, a labor union or an agricultural cooperative. In other instances, the candidate may have connections with the central government that might result in a new bridge for the district, or he may be in a position to facilitate access to government agencies of one kind or another. Here a vote is presumably being traded for a tangible benefit.

The three preferences proceed from the diffuse to the specific. In the first case, the voter is reacting to a diffuse patron-client relationship. In the second situation, the voter casts a vote for the candidate because he respects his achievements, but does not particularly expect anything in return.

Finally, in the third case, there is an expectation of a return, a quid pro quo.[9]

THE MOBILIZATION OF VOTERS

Voters may have preferences, but they do not exercise their votes in a vacuum. They are wooed by parties, organizations, and candidates. In short, they are mobilized. We have already seen that the two major parties do not have much in the way of local party organizations. In fact, they have sometimes been likened to an inverted pyramid—that is, large central organizations, but no supporting base at the local level. This means that neither the Liberal Democratic nor the Socialist candidate can rely on the party organization to help corral the votes for him. He must find some substitute machinery.

In those areas that are predominantly agricultural, removed from metropolitan areas and hence more immune to urbanizing influences, candidates are likely to link up directly or indirectly through intermediaries such as prefectural assemblymen with the local notables who control a certain number of votes. The notable is usually able to persuade his followers to vote for the candidate to whom he has pledged his support. This style of voter mobilization, however, is clearly on the decline. As was indicated in our discussion of recent changes in agriculture, the number of full-time farmers has dropped sharply as a result of the rapid economic growth that marked the decade of the 1960s.

The decline of the notable as a source of votes has forced conservative candidates to resort to a new strategy, namely, the creation of *koenkai* or "support groups." Liberal Democratic Diet members and politicians who are thinking of running in future elections have formed their personal machines. These are made up of relatives, friends, classmates, business associates and the like, plus *their* friends and relatives. Members join these support groups because of their personal ties with

[9] Scott C. Flanagan, "Voting Behavior in Japan," *Comparative Political Studies*, 1, 3 (October 1968), 393.

the Diet member or prospective candidate. Each member may be required to pay a nominal sum as dues, but he is likely to get back much more than what he has paid in in the form of drinks and food at parties and gatherings hosted by the politician. Although the support groups are most characteristic of the Liberal Democratic party politicians, it is said that some Socialists and even some leaders of the Clean Government party have established them.

Obviously, the mobilization of voters through the local notable and through support groups rests on personal ties. It presupposes widespread social networks based on kinship, friendship, business and professional associations, school ties, and so on—in short, a fairly stable population. But our demographic data tell us that during the 1960s more than half a million young men and women moved from the rural areas to the cities every year. Moreover, there was population movement within the big cities. Some observers have referred to the "doughnut" phenomenon: stability or decline of population in the central areas of the big city and rapid growth in surrounding suburban areas.

Mobility obviously removes an individual from the old social networks that functioned as channels for the mobilization of his vote. A newcomer to an area, unless he is one of the relatively few ideologues, is likely to take little interest in local politics and even in national politics. He will probably not even bother to go to the polls unless he finds some compelling personality running for office. It usually takes years for an individual to get enmeshed in the local social networks, and some, especially white collar workers who expect to change their place of residence every few years, may never consider themselves part of the community. Since young people are most likely to move around, one can understand why their participation rate is low.

There are, however, at least two ways in which these mobile individuals can be integrated into the political system. One is through local organizations that often have rather specific interests—for example, farmers' cooperatives, credit unions, youth associations, medical associations, shopkeepers' associations, PTAs, road safety councils, and so on. The other is through the local branches of the Clean Government party or the Communist Party.

As we have previously mentioned, both the Socialist and Democratic Socialist parties rely on their respective affiliated labor union federations. Since neither has much in the way of local party organizations, they are not involved in the everyday life of the workers. They have not succeeded in bringing socialism as an ideology and a political movement to the working class. Local union officials on whom the parties depend to bring out the vote are naturally busy with union affairs most of the time and have little time to engage in political education on behalf of the party.

Labor union members will ordinarily be active politically if one of the officials of their own union happens to be running for office. They would not be likely to work so hard for other Socialist candidates. Still, organized labor does manage to deliver a sizable block of votes to the Socialist and Democratic Socialist parties, and certainly the financial support that the unions give to the parties is crucial. However, as we have seen, organized labor accounts for only about 35 percent of all workers, and the rate of unionization has not risen over the years. Moreover, unionized workers represent the more privileged section of the working class; they are economically more secure, and their pay is higher. As we have suggested, there are some signs that with rapid economic growth and a steady rise in pay scales, embourgeoisement is taking place. As living standards rise, more and more workers are acquiring middle class self-images. Affluent workers may become more concerned about parking space at the plant than about working class solidarity and militancy against management.

Among the more conspicuous defectors from the Socialist cause in recent years are the young people. In the 1950s it was commonly said that when a young man or woman voted for the first time, he or she was more likely than not to cast a ballot for a Socialist or some other left-wing candidate. This is no longer the case. In its 1968 survey of national character, the Institute of Mathematical Statistics (Tokeisuri Kenkyujo) found that 25 percent of the respondents in the 20 to 24 age bracket supported the Socialist party; 5 percent supported the Democratic Socialists; and 3 percent, the Communists. Moreover, 31 percent reported that they supported no political party. Thus it appears that only a minority of the youth in their early twenties belong in the left-wing camp.

To summarize, the electorate may be thought of as being divided into three broad groups. The first would be those who identify with a particular political party. The sources of that party identification are no doubt varied. Some were socialized into a political party through their parents; some support a party because of ideological reasons. Still others have party preferences because of membership in social groups ranging all the way from the hamlet to labor unions, religious organizations, and the like. And, of course, in some individuals more than one of these factors may be at work.

The second group would be comprised of what some observers would call the "floating vote." As the label implies, this type of voter is not committed to a party or an individual. He is somewhat different from the independent voter in American politics in that he generally does not vote after a careful consideration of issues based on informed thinking. This type of vote is more frequently found in urban areas, where individuals can be more anonymous and free of community pressure. In terms of occupation, the "floating vote" is generally associated with white collar workers and with intellectuals. It is also more characteristic of youth than of the aged.

This type of voter may be associated with another phenomenon, the "sympathy vote." Sometimes a candidate will win an election by an overwhelming margin, while another candidate in the same party will just fail to get into the winner's circle. In the following election, a number of voters may switch to the one who in the last election barely failed to win out of sympathy for him, assuming that the one who had won by a large margin was a sure winner anyway. If enough voters reason this way, of course, the sure winner ends up a loser. There are certain districts where this happens with some regularity, and it would suggest that in those areas there are a substantial number of floating voters who are not committed to a particular candidate.

The third group of voters are those who have no party preference and are in the main not interested in politics. They are not likely to take the time and trouble to go to the polls unless some particularly attractive candidate appears or there is an issue that has aroused the public, such as evidence of bribery and corruption in politics. It is, of course, difficult to make an estimate of the proportion of these three groups within the electorate, and obviously the proportion would vary from time to time. What appears to be a reasonable estimate is one put forward by Shinohara: Those committed to a political party—40 percent; the floating vote—30 percent; no party preference—30 percent.[10]

VOTING AND THE ELECTION SYSTEM

Institutional arrangements invariably affect the way in which votes are cast and the distribution of party strength in the legislature. Single-member constituencies tend to favor the majority party, while proportional representation encourages the growth of minor parties. The present Japanese electoral system is neither a single-member constituency nor proportional representation, but falls somewhere in between.

For elections to the House of Representatives, the country is divided into 123 electoral districts, plus Okinawa. Each district, except one (Amami Islands), elects three, four, or five representatives, with a little less than twice the number of candidates running. (The number of candidates has declined steadily over the years, which may be taken as an indirect indication that party control over elections has been strengthened.) In order to be elected, a candidate must place in the top three to five, depending upon the size of the district. Each voter, however, writes in the name of only one candidate. Under this system, a successful candidate needs to have the support of only a minority of the voters in his district. Naturally, the number of votes necessary to be included among the top three to five depends upon the size of the electorate, the number of candidates running, and the spread of votes among them.

[10] Hajime Shinohara, "70-nen Dai to Kakushin no Kanosei" [The 1970s and the Potentialities of the Progressives], *Sekai*, 292 (March 1970), 34.

Because three to five candidates run in each district, it is essential from the party standpoint that the support it gets be distributed reasonably evenly among its candidates. For instance, if too many candidates are allowed to run, the vote will be spread too thin, with the result that some seats will be lost. A strong vote-getter can sometimes be a handicap because he will get too many votes at the expense of his running mates. Indeed, this competition between or among politicians for the vote in one district is one of the causes, although not a major one, of factionalism in Japanese parties. Men from the same district are virtually never in the same faction.

As we suggested earlier, the electoral system intervenes between voters and the party makeup in the lower house. In Great Britain the "cube law" is said to operate: The winning party's share of seats in the House of Commons varies as the cube of the proportion of its vote. That is, if the winning party gets twice as many votes as the losing party, it will win roughly eight times as many seats. In a multiparty system, this would not be true. The precise mathematical formula for the Japanese case has not been worked out, but it is evident that the system works in favor of the Liberal Democrats and at the same time allows as many as five parties to win representation.

First, let us take the proposition that the system helps the Liberal Democrats. We may begin by noting the urban-rural balance. The allocation of seats between rural and urban constituencies greatly favors the former, because the urban migration that persists year after year has not been fully taken into account. The present electoral system and basic allocation of seats was established in 1947, when the population in the cities still reflected the dispersal of persons into the rural areas during the war. Any reapportionment would have to hurt the Liberal Democrats; since they hold the majority, they are not about to sponsor it. The first and relatively minor readjustment did not occur until the 1967 election, when five new electoral districts were created, three in Tokyo, one in Aichi prefecture, and one in Osaka, representing 19 additional seats in the House of Representatives. Since no representatives were taken away from the rural districts that have been losing population, these districts are still very much overrepresented. The rural districts are typically the smaller three-man districts, with the result that the Liberal Democratic party can do better than its national vote would suggest, because a "party will win more (fewer) seats for a given share of vote, other things being equal, the greater its relative strength in small (large) constituencies."[11] For example, in the 1969 election, the Liberal Democrats won 47.6 percent of the national vote, but secured 59.3 percent of the seats in the lower house. The Communist Party represents the other extreme. The Communists run candidates everywhere, even in those districts where the possibility of victory is remote, because they look upon an election as an opportunity to advertise the party. Every candidate picks up some votes, however few, but many votes are wasted because the great majority of candidates lose. This is borne out by the ratios: The Communists in 1969 got 6.8 percent of the national vote, but only 2.9 percent of the seats. The other parties were in between, and their share of seats was somewhat smaller than the national vote.

The second point has to do with the fortunes of minor parties. Quite clearly, in a single-member constituency system it is difficult for minor parties to get established because they must win the highest percentage of votes among all the competing parties. As we have indicated, where you have multimember districts, as in Japan, it is easier, particularly in the larger five-man districts. Indeed, in recent years the Communist and Clean Government parties have done best in such districts. At the same time, it would appear that the maximum size of the electoral district, which is five members, would constrain further proliferation of minor parties.

[11] Duff Spafford, "The Electoral System of Canada," *American Political Science Review*, 64, 1 (March 1970), 171.

10 Political Violence

If one were to scratch beneath the surface of stable democracies, one would find a wide sharing of political goals and values as well as a strong commitment to the democratic "rules of the game." Because values are shared, individuals know what to expect of others, and there can be harmonious social interaction. In short, there exists a political community shrouded with an aura of moral rightness, and most people most of the time do what is considered to be right—for example, they obey the laws and pay taxes—because they have been socialized into the norms of the political community.

At the same time, one cannot deny that physical coercion, or the threat of it, is part and parcel of the political order. There is no government that does not have some kind of police force and a system of courts and jails to deal with those deemed to be acting contrary to existing social and political norms. Thus, all definitions of political systems contain the notion that there are agencies which have a monopoly of force and exercise it legitimately on behalf of the political community. For example, David Easton speaks of the political system as "interactions through which values are authoritatively allocated for a society."[1] Some analysts even make a distinction between force and violence: Force is looked upon as the legitimate use of coercion, violence is an illegitimate use.

[1] David Easton, *A Systems Analysis of Political Life* (New York: Wiley, 1965), p. 21.

POLITICAL VIOLENCE: ITS FORMS AND CAUSES

Regardless of whether or not political violence is considered legitimate, it is clear to anyone who regularly reads the newspapers that its incidence in many parts of the world is rather high, and perhaps even rising. There are, of course, many forms of political violence: assassination, coup d'etat, political kidnapping, mass demonstration, riot, civil war. The following classification scheme has been proposed by Ted Gurr: (1) turmoil, which would be violent outbreaks, more or less spontaneous, unorganized, and involving substantial numbers of people; (2) conspiracy, which would be highly organized and involve small numbers of people; and (3) internal war, which would be highly organized, involve wide popular participation, and would be aimed at overthrowing the regime by the use of violence.[2] If we apply this scheme to the Japanese case, we discover that virtually all the forms of political violence that have occurred in recent years would come under the "turmoil" category, and that the incidence of violence, if measured on an international scale, is actually on the low side. Yet, there are examples of violence of varying degrees of magnitude, and it would appear that violence has become, in some sense, a part of the Japanese political process. How and why is this so?

In *Why Men Rebel*, Gurr has attempted to explain political violence in a systematic way. He sees a three-stage causal sequence: (1) development of discontent; (2) the politicization of the discontent; and (3) the actualization of discontent against political actors and objects. According to this theory, discontent arises from a discrepancy between men's expectations and what they think they are capable of attaining, given the social conditions that exist. This discontent, however, must be politicized. Individuals are not likely to resort to violence unless they come to believe through political doctrines, ideologies, and other means that violence against the political authorities and institutions is both justified and useful in getting rid of the

[2] Ted Robert Gurr, *Why Men Rebel* (Princeton, N.J.: Princeton University Press, 1971), p. 11.

unsatisfactory conditions. But the question of whether or not political violence will actually break out will depend on the balance between the coercive control the political authorities will be able to exercise and the amount of institutional support the dissidents will be able to command.

When we turn to the Japanese scene, we find that most of the more notable examples of political violence have taken the form of large-scale demonstrations, which have often led to angry confrontations between the police, trained and equipped for antiriot work, and demonstrators, protected by helmets and armed with wooden staves and rocks. In these confrontations, occasionally someone is killed, numerous individuals are injured, and certainly as many as several hundred demonstrators end up in jail.

The famous series of demonstrations that occurred in May and June of 1960 in connection with the ratification of the Mutual Security Treaty with the United States and that led to the cancellation of President Eisenhower's proposed visit to Japan were the largest in scale to date. The most violent confrontation occurred on June 15, when thousands of demonstrators, many of them students, clashed with police trying to guard the several gates around the National Diet building. By the time the demonstration broke up about 4:30 a.m., hundreds of students and police had been injured, one girl was dead (she had been crushed by the crowd), 196 students had been arrested, and 10 police trucks had been totally destroyed.[3]

The tenor of more recent demonstrations is evident in the following list of incidents that occurred within one year (1967–1968):

October 1967: Several thousand demonstrators jammed the Haneda Airport in an effort to prevent the departure of Prime Minister Sato on a visit to Southeast Asia.

November 1967: Demonstration at Haneda Airport to try to prevent Prime Minister Sato from leaving for Washington, D.C.

January 1968: Demonstration at Sasebo Naval Base to try to

[3] George R. Packard, III, *Protest in Tokyo* (Princeton, N.J.: Princeton University Press, 1966), p. 297.

prevent the visit of the U.S.S. *Enterprise*, a nuclear-powered aircraft carrier.

February 1968: Demonstration to oppose the establishment of a U.S. Army field hospital in Oji, in northern Tokyo.

March 1968: Demonstration to oppose the proposed construction of a new international airport in Chiba prefecture.

October 1968: Demonstration at Shinjuku Station to protest the transportation by the Japanese railway system of oil for use by United States armed forces.

As we can see, most of the demonstrations are concerned with foreign policy issues rather than with problems in domestic politics. The demonstrators are expressing discontent with the foreign policy of the Japanese government, particularly the policy of continuing the military alliance with the United States. Since many of the demonstrations involve the more radical, Marxist-oriented college students, organized labor, and the left-wing political parties, we might assume that their opposition rests on ideological grounds—that is, on their perception of American foreign policy as being dictated by imperialistic drives and on their fear that Japan might become involved in an imperialistic war in Asia. Without discounting the ideological factor, we might point to another factor that is probably operating here. It has to do with the nature of discontent, and we can begin with college students, who are always involved in the major demonstrations.

Student disaffection has many sources. For instance, the structure and operation of universities leave much to be desired. Originally designed for elite education, Japanese colleges are now involved in mass education; they enroll about one-fifth of the youth of college age. In many instances the curriculum is outmoded, classes are large, and some students have complained that they went through college without ever having exchanged words with a professor. In order to pass the competitive entrance examinations, students had to go through what is popularly known as "examination hell," studying late into the night while in junior high school and high school and foregoing the pleasures that come from friendships and social life, so it is understandable that many should find college life a terrible letdown. An even more fundamental problem—and this is particularly true for the activists in the student movement—is the search for what students call "self-hood" (*shutaisei*). Some youths rebel against the constraints imposed on them by their families and by groups with which they are affiliated. They rebel against pressures for mass conformity and against the drive for material goods. And so, as Lifton has noted, "they respond strongly to those elements of Marxist thought which refer to self-realization."[4]

At the same time that they are rebelling, they are also searching for other groups with which they can affiliate, groups whose values would be different from those they oppose in society. The prime student organization became the Zengakuren (short for Zenkoku Gakusei Jichikai Rengo, All-Japan Federation of Student Self-government Associations), first organized in 1948. From the time of its formation until about 1958, Zengakuren leaders consisted mostly of student Communists. In 1958 student Communist leaders became disillusioned with the Japan Communist Party because of the controls the Party exercised over them and especially because of the shift in Party line to one of moderation, a change clearly dictated by Moscow. When those who opposed the Party were purged, they formed an anti-Japanese Communist Party organization known as the Communist League or "Bund." It was this organization that took an active part in the 1960 demonstrations. The failure of the 1960 demonstrations to prevent ratification of the treaty led to factional strife over the question of the evaluation of the 1960 strategy, and eventually the Bund broke up into three militantly radical organizations, which have sometimes fought against each other. Meanwhile, a pro-Communist Party Zengakuren was also formed, a moderate organization. The organized student movement is now badly splintered, and this may be one reason foreign policy issues are stressed: It is easier to get unified action against a foreign target.

A similar consideration may also be operating in the case of the involvement of organized labor in mass demonstrations in concert with student organizations. Labor union leaders, especially at the national federation level, are committed, in various

[4] Robert J. Lifton, "Youth and History," *Asian Cultural Studies*, 3 (October 1962), 124.

degrees, to Marxist ideology. It is highly doubtful that this commitment is widely shared by the rank and file of union members. For example, workers in a large industrial firm were once asked if they agreed with the following statements:

1. I support the Communist party or the left wing of the Socialist party.
2. I intend to remain a member of the working class in the future. (I don't want to become a capitalist or a member of the middle class.)
3. Labor and management should oppose each other, and not cooperate.
4. Labor unions should strive to promote the solidarity of the working class, rather than try to increase production.

Workers who have accepted Marxist ideology could be expected to reply affirmatively to all four questions. Yet in this survey, only 2 percent of all those interviewed did.[5] Still, left-wing individuals will often be elected to leadership positions within unions. One explanation is that this represents a symbolic act. That is, as we suggested in Chapter 4, enterprise unionism tends to encourage worker identification with the firm because workers who have a lifetime commitment to a firm want to see it prosper.

At the same time, although the spread of democratic ideals and the growth of unionism have weakened the authority and power of management, they have not destroyed it. Management is still in charge, and there is a conflict of interest between it and the workers. Many workers, however, find it difficult to openly oppose management and assert their rights, given paternalistic practices and the stress on harmony. Those who do openly fight management need a radical ideology to give them moral backing, and those who do not sometimes give vent to their discontent by engaging in political protests outside. As Robert E. Cole sees it, "political activity in unions has multiple purposes and multiple consequences. Worker participation in political demonstrations . . . must be understood as an

[5] Chikio Hayashi *et al.*, *Nihonjin no Kokuminsei* [National Character of the Japanese] (Tokyo: Shiseido, 1965), pp. 36–38.

expressive act designed to call attention to worker discontent at being the 'outs' and not as instrumental action designed to secure the fixed goal of revolution."[6] If this interpretation is correct, then one would have to say that the ultimate goals of political violence are different for student radicals, who seek to usher in a new kind of social order, and most sections of organized labor.

VIOLENCE AND THE POLITICAL PROCESS

The third of the participant groups in political demonstrations are the left-wing political parties, especially the Socialist and the Communist. For these organizations, the goals sought through violent behavior may well be different from those of the radical students and organized labor, although it is true that all three groups, at least at the leadership level, share a preference for a common ideology, namely Marxism. It would appear that left-wing opposition parties often look upon street demonstrations as well as the use of force within the halls of the National Diet as an adjunct to the more normal processes of debate and voting on legislative bills.

The nature of opposition politics in Japan has been conditioned by at least two factors: The inability of the opposition to get periodical control of the government and the place of majority rule in the Japanese conception of democracy. As was shown in Chapter 8, the party system has operated in such a way that since the end of the war, the Liberal Democratic party and its predecessors have exercised power virtually continuously. In this sense, the Japanese situation is different from that which has prevailed in Great Britain, where from time to time the Labor party has managed to overwhelm the Tories at the polls. Because the Left has been relegated to the position of a permanent opposition with no immediate prospect of coming to power, it cannot afford to take a relaxed and tolerant view toward issues about which the intensity of feeling among opposition groups runs high. Examples of such issues would be

[6] Robert E. Cole, "Japanese Workers, Unions, and the Marxist Appeal," *The Japan Interpreter,* 6 (Summer 1970), 126–27.

those related to the so-called "reverse course," that is, measures that would suggest a revival of prewar authoritarian institutions and practices. If an opposition party felt its chances of winning the next election were good, it would be more tolerant of legislative proposals because once it got control of the government as a result of victory at the polls, it could conceivably repeal laws it felt were repugnant. But since in Japan the possibility of repealing legislation enacted by the conservatives is not a viable one, the left-wing opposition parties are moved to use extraparliamentary measures to resist unpalatable legislative proposals.

Moreover, resistance, even to the extent of using force, is encouraged by the conflict between the principle of majority rule inherent in democracy and the traditional notion of consensus. Typically, decision making in a small group situation where group members know each other well proceeds as follows: Everyone informally gives his views, and after much talk in a relaxed atmosphere and a good deal of give and take, a consensus eventually emerges in which not everyone agrees 100 percent with what is being decided, but even those who were in the minority feel that they can live with the decision. Such a procedure, of course, would not work in large groups made up of many individuals with diverse views and interests, and so decision making tends to be dominated by the leadership and carried out on the basis of majority rule. When majority rule is carried out without maximum consultation and satisfactory incorporation of minority views, the usual response is to criticize the proceedings as "undemocratic."

In American congressional politics, elaborate rules (a requirement for a two-thirds majority in some cases) and procedures (the filibuster) have been worked out to protect the position of minority groups who feel strongly about their cause; but in Japanese legislative practice, such institutionalized devices have not yet come into existence. The result is that left-wing opposition groups have taken to such strong-arm methods as blocking the aisles to prevent the Speaker from getting to the rostrum, and the conservatives have responded by bringing in the police to forcibly eject the opposition. For example, in October 1958 Nobusuke Kishi, then prime minister, introduced a bill to enlarge the powers of the police to engage in preventive action, including interrogation, search, and arrest. The opposition parties vehemently opposed the bill on grounds that it would make Japan into a police state. In order to get the bill enacted, the government needed to extend the Diet session, which the Socialists tried to prevent by surrounding the Speaker's rostrum. The government's response was to have the Vice-Speaker pass the extension from the floor of the House of Representatives. Having failed to block the extension, the opposition mobilized union workers, students, and political activists and launched a series of strikes and mass demonstrations. The tactic proved to be successful, because the government decided not to force the issue (there was also dissension within the ranks of the ruling party), and withdrew the bill.

One of the consequences of the 1960 demonstrations was the adoption of the so-called low posture policy by Hayato Ikeda, who succeeded Kishi as prime minister. Until his resignation because of illness in 1964, Mr. Ikeda took pains to avoid proposing legislative and other measures that were certain to provoke the wrath of the opposition parties and possibly lead to mass demonstrations in the streets. It is clear that the threat of violence in the legislative halls followed by mass demonstrations outside has deterred the ruling party from seeking to carry out some measures which it favors. For example, some conservatives have from time to time indicated their desire to change the electoral system from the present one of multiple candidates to a single-member, simple-majority system. Since the Liberal Democrats are the largest single party, a single-member constituency system would add substantially to the majority the party enjoys in the lower house. To date, the government has not attempted to change the system, despite the advantages it would bring, because it is fully aware that all the opposition parties, knowing that they would be hurt by it, would ultimately take to the streets. Presumably, the government, in weighing the electoral advantages against the political turmoil that would ensue, decided the price was too high. In opting for democracy, men have decided that debate and ballots are preferable to fisticuffs and bullets for settling political differences. Nevertheless, there is lurking in the background the implicit assumption that the ultimate weapon in politics is force.

11 Public Policy Outputs

In the preceding chapters we have looked at Japanese politics from a variety of angles—social structure, political attitudes, institutions, pressure groups, and political parties—on the assumption that by looking at the parts we can get some appreciation of the political system as a whole. So far, however, we have not addressed ourselves to the important question of the consequences. Does the character of the political system one lives under make a difference? Does the political system, in the last analysis, affect the quality of life? Stated more precisely, what are the payoffs in terms of public policy?

It is a curious fact that despite their obvious importance, public policy outputs have not been studied very much in a systematic way—with some reason. For one thing, outputs cover an amazing range of activities. Taxation systems, which extract resources from the population; regulatory laws, which affect everything from the kind of cars one can buy to relations with foreign countries; and distribution measures, which affect the allocation of resources for such things as social welfare, education, roads, dams, and the like all come under the heading of system outputs.[1] Then there is the problem of sheer volume. Official actions, including laws, regulations, and ordinances enacted by governments at various levels, national and local, are likely to reach a staggering figure every year. In Japan the central government publishes every day of the year, except

[1] Gabriel A. Almond and G. Bing Powell, Jr., *Comparative Politics: A Developmental Approach* (Boston: Little, Brown, 1966), Chap. 8.

Sundays and holidays, an Official Gazette, which serves as a public announcement of government actions taken during that day. Everything from texts of international treaties to announcements of transfer of personnel from one office to another is included. The bound volume for each month may run well over 1,000 large pages printed in four columns. For example, the December 1970 volume contains the texts of 145 laws enacted by the National Diet, 354 Cabinet orders issued by the prime minister for the purpose of implementing legislation, 48 regulations emanating from the Prime Minister's Office, and 29 regulations issued by the various ministries. All this suggests that in Japan, as in virtually every other modern state, the government is closely involved in the everyday life of the citizen. The very scope of this involvement makes it difficult to study the phenomenon empirically and systematically. Hence what follows must necessarily be sketchy and impressionistic.

CENTERS OF DECISION MAKING

Most observers of the Japanese political scene will probably agree that two decision-making centers exert a powerful influence on the character of public policy in Japan. They are the political parties operating at the cabinet and Diet levels, and the bureaucracy entrenched in the ministries and agencies.

Given the present party structure, quite clearly the ruling Liberal Democratic party, to the extent that its faction leaders are able to agree on public policy issues, overshadows the opposition parties. Perhaps the remarkable thing, however, is the amount of accommodation that has been reached between the ruling party and the opposition. The record of the 58th Diet session (spring 1968) reveals, for example, that a total of 95 government-sponsored bills passed the House of Representatives. On these bills, the Democratic Socialist and the Clean Government parties voted with the government more than 80 percent of the time, and even the Socialist party voted for two-thirds of the bills. Only the Communist Party indicated its opposition stance by voting almost three-fourths of the time against the government's legislative program. Out of the 95 bills passed, in only 11 cases did all opposition parties present a united front and vote no, and about one-half of these instances had to do with changes in the tax laws. Incidentally, in the same session, only 9 bills sponsored by Diet members were approved, which shows the extent to which legislation is controlled by the party leaders, especially those in the cabinet. The average backbencher spends most of his time running errands for voters from his constituency and has little to do with the legislative program. He is, however, expected to turn out and vote for those bills sponsored by his party. He cannot vote against his party's bills, and in those rare instances when he feels he cannot support his party, he will be absent from the floor when the vote is taken.

Actually, much of the legislation that is passed originates in some government agency. This is as true today as it was in the past, for as we have suggested elsewhere, the Japanese bureaucracy historically has taken the lead in modernizing the country. R. P. Dore's study of the enactment of the Factory Law in 1911 provides us with a handy illustration of the initiative exercised by the civil service.[2]

As was true in England, during the early phases of industrialization in Japan factory workers were terribly exploited, forced to work long hours under conditions which were often injurious to health and conducive to a high accident rate. Every factory owner was free to impose whatever conditions he saw fit. The industrialists, of course, were either unenthusiastic or even openly hostile to the idea of government regulation of factory conditions. Since labor was not organized into unions, it was not in a position to agitate for factory legislation. Even if the workers had organized and brought pressure to bear, it is doubtful that the politicians would have sided with them. The enactment of the factory law was chiefly the work of civil servants, who had the support of a small number of socialistically inclined intellectuals. It was certainly not the result of interest group pressure on politicians.

A more recent example is the "income doubling plan" associ-

[2] R. P. Dore, "The Modernizer as a Special Case: Japanese Factory Legislation, 1882–1911," *Comparative Studies in Society and History,* 11, 4 (October 1969), 437.

ated with the late Hayato Ikeda, prime minister from 1960 to 1964. In 1961 Ikeda announced a plan whereby Japan would seek sufficient economic growth during the 1960s to enable the country to double its national income by 1970. Actually, the plan was not a brainchild of the Prime Minister, but was conceived by the Economic Planning Agency, which is part of the Office of the Prime Minister, and is somewhat comparable to the Council of Economic Advisers in the United States. The Economic Planning Agency is close to the Ministry of International Trade and Industry, since many of its personnel have come from MITI. It appears that the Ministry of International Trade and Industry backed the income doubling plan because it disagreed with the Ministry of Finance, which had proposed liberalization of trade and of control over foreign exchange. The Ministry of International Trade and Industry, which tends to be strongly protectionist and committed to promoting Japan's competitive position in the world economy, opposed liberalization unless it went hand-in-hand with economic growth and structural change. For example, MITI for a long time opposed the entry of American auto manufacturers into Japan until such time as the Japanese auto industry had been strengthened through the merger of a number of small companies into larger companies able to compete effectively with such giants as General Motors.

Thus, policy making in the Japanese political system is not always in response to inputs from interest groups. To be sure, the bureaucracy is undoubtedly sensitive to demands from well-organized and determined pressure groups; but it also makes policy in accordance with some goals—say, the public interest or the national interest—held by the bureaucrats. The example also suggests that the bureaucracy is not a monolithic entity, but is rather made up of subgroups whose goals may not always coincide. And sometimes it is the competition and conflict within a pluralistic bureaucracy that leads to policy initiatives.

ORGANIZED INTERESTS AND PUBLIC POLICY

As we have suggested, bureaucrats and party leaders exert a great influence on public policy, but there are instances in which those outside the elite group can be effective. Under certain conditions, the elite can be persuaded or even compelled to adopt policies it may not particularly favor. If a sizable number of individuals have a common grievance, they may be able to organize for the purpose of seeking a political solution to their problem. To be successful, the group will need good leadership, a workable strategy, and—above all—political clout. A good example of this is the successful effort of the ex-landlords to secure compensation for some of their losses (described in Chapter 6).

There are other groups that actually or potentially could secure gains for themselves through organized political action. In the past veterans have succeeded in getting restored to them pensions denied them by the Occupation. Doctors, working through their medical association, have sought to get the fees paid them through the national health insurance system raised to higher levels. Probably in the future consumer groups will become more active in promoting their interests through political pressure and action.

An interesting aspect of the question of organized interests and public policy are those instances where organized action does not take place. Higher education would be a good example. A college diploma is becoming increasingly important if a person wants to achieve high social status and secure a good income. There has therefore been tremendous social pressure to secure admission to universities, especially the prestigious government institutions. The universities, both government and private, have responded to this pressure by extending their enrollments, but there has not been the kind of large-scale expansion that has occurred in the United States, especially at the community-supported junior college and state-supported university levels. Since a large number of families have college-age (or potentially college-age) children, one would have thought that they would form a large pressure group seeking to force the government to appropriate funds both to expand existing universities and to establish many new ones. But this has not happened. Each family tries to get its own sons and daughters into college by hiring private tutors and taking other means to increase the possibility of their passing the competitive entrance examinations. In short, each family looks for an individual solution instead of a collective solution through organized political pressure. As we shall see later, there are other examples of a lack of collective effort to solve problems.

PURSUIT OF THE GENERAL WELFARE

We can anticipate that groups with special interests, especially economic, will try to influence public policy in a direction beneficial to them. As we have suggested above, not all groups will get what they seek. One reason is that scarce resources must be allocated in some way. Another is that demands made by competing groups sometimes cancel each other out. For instance, a taxpayers' group seeking economy in government and a specialized lobby pressuring for increased appropriations cannot be accommodated at the same time. Some cynics might say that it is this competition among conflicting groups that preserves the public interest, and they may well be right. However it is preserved, the public interest is an integral part of politics. When large numbers of people begin to feel that the common good, the public interest, the general welfare have gone by the wayside, the legitimacy of the political system is threatened, and that system may be in for trouble.

To say that it is necessary to have a conception of the public interest is not to argue that what constitutes the public interest is everywhere the same. Like so many things in politics, it depends on the basic attitudes that are widely shared among the people. In Japanese politics, notions about the general welfare are more clearly developed in terms of the local community than at the national level. One indication of this is the greater interest citizens generally show in local matters and the higher turnout in local compared to national elections. But even in community affairs, interest tends to be limited to long-time residents, and it may take as long as ten years before a person who moves into a community begins to feel a sense of involvement in what is happening to it.

There are examples of local citizens banding together in pursuit of political objectives. The uncovering of flagrant cases of corruption on the part of city councilmen, for example, stimulated the organization of a citizen's movement, with mass meetings and the circulation of petitions, that eventually led to an attempt to recall the guilty politicians or defeat them in the next election. There have also been cases where local citizens have come into open conflict with town or city governments over the issue of industrial development in their localities. Local politicians will often seek to attract new industries into their area in the hope of expanding the tax base, only to run into opposition on the part of the residents. Proposals to build oil refineries, chemical plants, and even power-generating facilities have been nullified because of political action on the part of citizens who feared that their environment would be further polluted.

As we have suggested, there is much less inclination to work together politically at the national level in order to enhance the general welfare. This is perhaps not altogether surprising, given the patron-client character of Japanese society. In such a society, there is a marked tendency to seek personal or group solutions to problems rather than collective remedies through action by the state. This is illustrated in Table 8 by citing comparative statistics on taxes and social security expenditures in relation to the gross national product which show that Japan spends much less than the Western European nations and the United States.

Table 8: Relation of Taxes and Social Security Expenditures to GNP

Japan (1966)	23.5%
West Germany (1963)	44.5
France (1963)	47.3
Italy (1963)	39.7
Great Britain (1963)	36.5
United States (1963)	33.9

Source: *Kosei Hakusho,* [White Paper on Welfare] 1968 ed., p. 17.

Corroborative evidence may be found in other kinds of data. For example, London, Manchester, Stockholm, and Chicago enjoy complete underground sewage systems, while only 44 percent of Tokyo is provided with underground sewage disposal.

The same sort of situation exists in relation to park facilities. Washington, D.C., boasts some 45 square meters of parks per resident (a very high figure); Amsterdam has 14; New York and Moscow almost 12 and 11, respectively; whereas Tokyo has a mere 1 square meter.

It is quite clear that so far the Japanese have not paid much attention to the question of the quality of life. One reason is that for a long time Japan was a relatively poor country, and it does take some degree of affluence before one begins to think of the amenities. Another reason is that the Japanese as a people are willing to put up with living conditions that people in other countries might simply refuse to accept. An American expert who recently saw pulp effluent being dumped into a river near Tokyo is quoted as having remarked: "I never imagined that it could be this bad. This goes beyond the bounds of mere pollution. It's unparalleled anywhere in the world! The local people must be very patient if they can put up with this and not get violent."[3]

Now that Japan has attained sufficient economic growth to become a nation with the third highest GNP in the world, an awareness of the need to shift priorities is developing. In the summer of 1970, pollution became a national issue. This was no doubt stimulated in part by the concern for pollution in the United States and other nations, because Japan is a country which is very sensitive to developments abroad, especially in the advanced nations. When Ralph Nader paid a visit to Japan, he found receptive audiences wherever he went, and there is evidence that he shook up the Japanese. The environment has been badly polluted, and when the situation is so bad that policemen sometimes have to wear gas masks and vending machines have been installed so that one can buy a whiff of oxygen, it does not take much of a stimulus to get people aroused.

The mass media helped to articulate the concern many people felt about their deteriorating environment by printing numerous articles on the subject of pollution. These were augmented by a flood of books that dissected the problem from various

[3] Yoshiro Kunimoto, "Pollution and Local Government," *Japan Quarterly*, 18, 2 (April–June 1971), 163.

points of view. The government was forced into the position of having to respond to public opinion, and so when the Prime Minister was queried by newspapermen, he said he would establish a new agency to deal with the problem. As a result, the Central Environmental Pollution Countermeasures Headquarters was organized on July 31, 1970, and placed under the jurisdiction of the Prime Minister's Office. The Ministries of Welfare, International Trade and Industry, Construction, Local Autonomy, and the Economic Planning Agency contributed personnel.

It is interesting that the formation of an ad hoc agency of this kind had the effect of galvanizing the old-line ministries into action. Government agencies everywhere try to defend their bailiwicks against intruders and also seek to retain their budgetary allocations and personnel. A new agency concerned with pollution represented a threat, and so the old agencies came up with legislative proposals that would ensure them a share in the business of fighting pollution. As a result, 14 bills initially put forward by various agencies and intended to control pollution passed the 64th extraordinary session of the National Diet (December 1970). Here is an example of legislative output emerging in response to a widely felt need. The case also illustrates the importance of government agencies taking the initiative in formulating public policy. It would appear that in many instances the pursuit of the general welfare depends less on abstract concern about the common good than on practical bureaucratic considerations of agency influence, power, and the size of the budget. But in any case, whatever the motive, considerations about the general welfare are not completely ignored.

In making such an observation, however, we ought not minimize the ability of vested interests to obstruct the pursuit of the common good. For example, one of the 14 antipollution bills was drafted by the Ministry of Justice, and its purpose was to make pollution a crime. In the bill was a provision which stated: "Any person who . . . produces a substance injurious to human health or creates a condition that may endanger the lives and persons of the public . . . shall be punished by a penal servitude of not more than three years or a fine of not more than 3 million yen." The business interests strongly opposed the bill on the ground that it would slow down Japan's economic growth. Despite opposition from the business community, the Prime Minister approved the bill, but it was modified by the Liberal Democratic party's Policy Council, which eliminated a key phrase, "or creates a condition that may endanger the lives and persons of the public," a change that significantly weakened the force of the legislation.

There is the added problem of enforcement. As we all know, public policy outputs represented by legislation do not tell the whole story. It is one thing to have laws on the books, and quite another thing to have them enforced vigorously by the various administrative agencies and by the courts. Public problems such as pollution, which affect powerful economic interests, are not going to be solved quickly in a straightforward manner. We can expect at best a zigzag course with numerous advances and retreats, especially in the absence of strong public interest lobbies actively working for the general welfare.

IN SUMMARY

David Easton has suggested that we should view politics as a kind of conversion process in which inputs in the form of demands and support are converted by the authorities into outputs, which in turn through feedback processes become new inputs.[4] In the Japanese political system, under some circumstances, as in the case of the dispossessed landlords cited earlier, the authorities do respond to demands and convert them into outputs. It is by being responsive to groups with political clout, such as rural voters, or with economic resources, such as large business firms, that the political elite is able to engender powerful political support for itself. In no democratic system can the elite in power afford to alienate those who support it either through votes or money.

But the substance of Japanese politics involves more than

[4] David Easton, *A Systems Analysis of Political Life* (New York: Wiley, 1965), pp. 349ff.

the conversion of demands into outputs by the authorities. Japanese democracy rests on a society that is based fundamentally on patron-client relationships. Most citizens relate to the political system through patrons or mediating agents—local notables, agricultural association officials, labor union leaders, party politicians. Much of the time, demands expressed through the patrons take the form of political action seeking particularistic benefits for the community (such as roads, bridges, schools, hospitals) or for individuals (such as jobs and intercession with government agencies). As we have suggested, such a society tends not to generate consistent and large-scale demands for broad public policy outputs based on ideological preferences. Rather, public policy rests on pragmatic considerations and is in this sense quite flexible.

The political system thus affords the authorities substantial leeway. Perhaps the key factor in the Japanese system is the powerful influence exerted by the bureaucrats who staff the government ministries and agencies. The role of a bureaucracy recruited strictly on the basis of achievement criteria and not subjected to a spoils system controlled by political parties is particularly vital in any democratic system that rests on a patron-client type of social system. Without the presence of such a bureaucracy, politics is likely to degenerate into a scrabble for pork-barrel benefits, and when that occurs, as it does, for example, in Philippines' politics, such matters as the pursuit of national development goals and the enhancement of the general welfare become nothing more than pious slogans. It is worth noting in this connection that the Japanese bureaucracy has a long tradition of commitment to development goals, and that even today, when Japan has become an advanced industrial power, the civil servants in the Ministry of International Trade and Industry and other agencies concerned with economic affairs continue to exercise a guiding hand in the economy to make sure that rapid economic growth will continue.

Indeed, rapid economic growth has been the overriding national goal in the postwar period. Although it is true that this goal has been pursued most vigorously by a coalition of business interests and the government bureaucracy, it has had the tacit, if not active, support of probably the majority of the people, whose incomes in real terms have risen despite the continuing inflation. However, as we have suggested, perhaps the time has come when a reordering of priorities must be attempted. Economic growth, when achieved at the expense of the quality of life, may become increasingly undesirable. As is true with most things in life, there is a price to be paid for almost everything one wishes to gain. The Japanese cannot expend large sums to improve the environment and increase social services and at the same time maintain an exceptionally high rate of economic growth. Somewhere along the line some choices will have to be made. Undoubtedly the bureaucracy will play a key role in making them, but in the long run choices that are unpopular with the general public are not likely to be viable. In this broad sense, Japanese democracy is no different from democracy in other parts of the world.

12 Japan in the 1970s

In the spring of 1941, the Japanese Foreign Minister, Yosuke Matsuoka, sent a telegram to his ambassador in Washington instructing him to convey to the American leaders the idea that it would be futile to go to war with Japan. Matsuoka's argument was that "even if America could make Japan surrender, and enforce a cruel treaty upon the Japanese people that might be comparable with the Versailles Treaty, Japan would break off such fetters or bonds within thirty years." To be sure, the victorious allied nations did not impose a cruel treaty, but it is also true that in 1945 an exhausted Japan lay prostrate. Certainly no one at that time predicted that Japan would reemerge within a relatively short time as an important nation in the world community, but subsequent history has vindicated Matsuoka's faith and confidence in the ability of the Japanese people to overcome adversity. His prediction was borne out.

Japan's economic recovery, characterized by some as an "economic miracle," has in recent times given rise to speculation as to her probable role in the future. An extreme example of this kind of speculation is Herman Kahn's book, *The Emerging Japanese Superstate.*[1] Mr. Kahn's thesis is that by the year 2000 Japan will surpass the most advanced Western nations in the size of her GNP, that given this great economic and financial power, she will seek to exercise political and/or military power

[1] Herman Kahn, *The Emerging Japanese Superstate: Challenge and Response* (Englewood Cliffs, N.J.: Prentice-Hall, 1970). A more moderate view is presented in Robert Guillain, *The Japanese Challenge: the Race to Year 2000* (Philadelphia: Lippincott, 1970).

commensurate with her economic capability, and finally that Japan will acquire nuclear weapons. People everywhere still have vivid memories of the Japanese attempt to seize control of vast sections of Asia through military conquest in the 1940s, and the emergence of an economically powerful Japan quite naturally gives rise to fears of a revival of Japanese militarism and expansion.

It is perhaps futile to try to predict what Japan will be like in the year 2000, but an attempt to assess probable developments in the 1970s on the basis of projections of recent trends would appear to be a feasible undertaking. Our discussion in this chapter will be centered on three interrelated problems: economic growth, the future of democracy, and Japanese foreign policy.

ECONOMIC GROWTH

In fiscal 1969 (April 1, 1969, to March 31, 1970), Japan's GNP increased 12.6 percent in real terms over 1968. It was by no means the largest increase since 1955. When an economy grows at that rate, it will double in approximately six years. By contrast, the American economy which grows at something like 4 percent a year, would require about eighteen years to double. As a consequence of the differential rate of growth, the Japanese economy would have grown at the end of eighteen years to 8 times its original size. Predictions by Kahn and others that the Japanese economy could overtake the American economy by the end of this century are based on this power of compound growth. The predictions, however, are quite clearly based on the assumption that the Japanese will be able to maintain consistently the kind of growth they have enjoyed during the last fifteen years. The question is whether we are warranted in making such an assumption.

There are at least five factors that can be cited to help explain Japan's postwar economic growth. They are:

1. The transformation of a semideveloped economy into a more mature one. This involves, among other things, a shift from

light to heavy industry and from agriculture to manufacturing and service industries, where productivity is substantially higher.

2. Large-scale technological borrowing from abroad. Instead of investing large sums in research and development, Japanese industries chose to acquire new technology from the more advanced countries through licensing and royalty payment arrangements. Even today, the amount Japan pays to foreign countries is much larger than what is received from the sale of Japanese technology to others.
3. Large-scale capital investment, much of it by private firms, in plant modernization. This was made possible by a high rate of savings, particularly by individuals, and by a low rate of taxation.
4. Availability of raw materials from abroad at reasonable prices and access to foreign markets, which produced the foreign exchange necessary to pay for essential imports.
5. A working partnership between government and business. Government has actively sought to promote rapid economic growth through regulation, loans, subsidies, fiscal management, and other measures.

It is doubtful that over the long run these conditions will persist. First, it is true that in certain respects the Japanese economy is still underdeveloped; for instance, there is the continued survival of small-scale farming and of small family-owned and operated business and manufacturing establishments. Shifts of manpower on a large scale from the less productive to the more productive sectors of the economy, as has been the case in recent years, cannot go on indefinitely. There will also be the problem of the shortage of labor. The age composition of the population is such that by 1985 the proportion of the population under 14 years of age will drop to about 21 percent of the population, in contrast to 25 percent in 1965. Moreover, there is a tendency for youth to stay in school longer as families get more affluent. Japan has already experienced labor shortages, which in turn have exerted upward pressure on wages. She is no longer a country with an abundant supply of cheap labor, and it is likely that wage rates will rise even faster than productivity. At the same time that the proportion of young people will be declining, the ratio of those 65 years of age and older within the population will climb; by 1985, this group will account for almost 10 percent of the total population. The aged will have to be taken care of, probably through a combination of contributions by the family and by the state.

Second, it seems unlikely that in the future the more advanced nations will be so willing to make available to Japanese firms new technology which will have the effect of making Japanese competition that much more intense. Both Japanese firms and the government will have to invest more money than before in research and development.

Third, between 1955 and 1965, the Japanese saved on the average of 25 percent of the net national product.[2] Among the reasons cited for this propensity to save are the desire to purchase modern durable consumer goods, for instance, TV sets, cars, refrigerators, and to provide for the education of the young. The consumption of nondurables—for example, food—has not risen all that much in the past. However, it is true that dietary preferences are changing, and as time goes on it is likely that people will insist on eating better. In addition, will they be willing to continue to live in cramped quarters, or will they want bigger apartments and homes? In short, it would seem likely that the exceptionally high rate of savings will not continue indefinitely into the future.

Fourth, industrial raw materials—petroleum, iron ore, copper, bauxite—have so far been readily available, and those nations that produce them have been more than willing to sell them to Japan. But the supply is not inexhaustible. Already there is talk of an eventual shortage of fossil fuels. Japan has been getting the great bulk of its petroleum, the demand for which has been growing rapidly, from the Middle East. The Japanese are aware that their supply could be cut off as a result of the political turmoil in that part of the world, and so they are making every effort to diversify their sources by investing in the development of oil in Indonesia, Australia, and other countries. It is also true that

[2] Tuvia Blumenthal, *Saving in Postwar Japan* (Cambridge, Mass.: East Asian Research Center, Harvard University, 1970), p. 5.

over the years the proportion of GNP accounted for by exports and imports has dropped. For instance, in 1969 exports plus imports came to only about 17 percent of GNP, so Japan is not all that dependent any more on foreign trade. But it still remains true that the country does not have a domestic supply of crucial raw materials and must depend on foreign sources.

Fifth, the government has been actively involved in promoting economic growth, and business for its part has been willing to accept government intervention to an extent that would be unthinkable in the United States. Government and business find it possible to work together because, as we have suggested in earlier chapters, the business community provides financial backing for the ruling Liberal Democratic party. Moreover, retired bureaucrats now hold important positions within the party, which helps to tie together the party and the bureaucracy. Finally, bureaucrats and business executives are linked by common social backgrounds and university ties as well as by economic ties forged through the employment of retired civil servants by business firms. Thus party, bureaucracy, and business form a trinity, a coalition bound by a common objective, namely, to enhance the economic power of the country. The continuation of such a coalition, of course, will depend on the ability of the conservative Liberal Democratic party to maintain itself in power. This leads us to the next problem, the survival of parliamentary democracy in the 1970s.

PARLIAMENTARY DEMOCRACY

Even a cursory survey of the types of political regimes that exist in the world today would show that viable parliamentary democracies represent a minority. It appears that certain conditions must be met if stable democracy is to endure for an extended period of time. What are some of these conditions?

First, there must be an underlying social consensus that is reflected in a homogeneous political culture. This does not mean that no cleavages can exist, for there are bound to be social differences and conflicts of one kind or another. The important point is that these cleavages are such that they can be bridged.

History has shown that certain kinds of cleavages are particularly difficult to bridge. Some that come to mind are religious cleavages and ethnic or communal cleavages. Religious and ethnic differences are particularly difficult to resolve because they are often perceived to be nonbargainable. As we have suggested elsewhere, the Japanese are not plagued by problems of this kind.

Second, the parliamentary regime must be perceived as legitimate by both the members of the elite and the masses. Every regime has a structure of authority, of command and obedience, and when the system is working well and brings benefits to the many, the overwhelming majority of the citizens will feel that they have a stake in the regime. The sense of legitimacy, of course, tends to be strengthened by the passage of time. Like everything else, individuals have to learn to play their political roles. In every system, the young are socialized into the on-going political arrangements that prevail. It is easy to see that continuity in the patterns of political socialization is important. By the same token, the longer a parliamentary system has been in operation, the better its chances of survival in the face of adversity. The present system is relatively young, but it does have something of a tradition; the first Parliament met in 1890, and the formation of the first political parties preceded the formation of the Parliament by about two decades. By Western standards, the Japanese parliamentary system is of rather recent origin, but no other country in Asia can claim even that much of a history.

This brings us to the third point, that is, the role of political parties in parliamentary politics. The experience of the developed democracies suggests that they are ruled "by party or factional coalitions that represent a fairly consistent social base, formed of coalitions of reasonably compatible interests."[3] As we suggested earlier, a broad kind of consensus does seem to exist among parties in Japan. In many countries socioeconomic issues provide the basis for ideological debate, but such issues are not all that important in Japan. The conservatives

[3] Andrew J. Milnor (ed.), *Comparative Political Parties* (New York: Crowell, 1969), p. 50.

do not oppose social welfare programs, as witnessed by the fact that they established a national health insurance program; they have accepted the existence of a nationalized railway system; and they have encouraged economic planning and government intervention in the economy. There are not many issues in the economic field that are irreconcilable and prevent the government and the opposition from working together much of the time. The data presented earlier on the extent of the accommodation achieved between the ruling party and the opposition in the field of legislation would seem to substantiate this interpretation.

Our discussion of parliamentary democracy therefore leads us to the conclusion that it is highly likely to maintain itself in the 1970s, barring some unforeseen cataclysmic economic or international crisis. We can anticipate, however, some shifts in relative party strength, although the shift will probably not be of sufficient magnitude to threaten the dominant position of the ruling Liberal Democratic party. Our projections of relative party support are shown in Table 9.

Table 9: Estimated Growth of Parties (in millions)

Year	Liberal Democratic	Socialist	Democratic Socialist	Clean Government	Communist	Total
1969	22.3	10.0	3.6	5.1	3.2	44.2*
1980	20.0	11.0	4.0	8.0	6.0	49.0*

* Excluding votes for minor parties and independent candidates.

If these projections are reasonably accurate, it is evident that the Liberal Democratic party will continue to be the largest single party, but its share of the vote will probably drop to about 40 percent. However, because of the nature of the electoral system that intervenes, the conservatives will probably be able to maintain a majority in the National Diet. Although at the local level the opposition has won control in some areas, this is not likely to take place at the national level. The present system of a dominant party and a divided opposition will probably continue through the 1970s.

In the event that this prediction turns out to be wrong and a multiparty system emerges, what kind of a coalition is likely? Assuming that the present party lineup remains, the question is who are the most likely coalition partners for the Liberal Democrats? There are some who suggest that if the Liberal Democrats get very much weaker, the party will split into a left and right wing, and there will be a realignment of the party system. It would seem that such a split is improbable, partly because the business interests who support the party would not welcome it. If we assume that the Liberal Democrats will stay intact, the most probable coalition partner would be the Democratic Socialists, followed by the Clean Government party. As we have seen, these two parties have been voting together with the Liberal Democrats in the House of Representatives about 80 percent of the time, so there should be little difficulty in forming a coalition if the Liberal Democrats reach a point where they no longer hold a majority. In short, we can envisage incremental change that will slowly shift votes away from the ruling party, but it will be some years before the cumulative shift will reach a point where it will make a significant difference in the composition of the leaders who run the country.

JAPANESE FOREIGN POLICY

Finally, we need to take a look at foreign policy, which in the past has been closely related to the program of rapid economic growth, and political dominance by the Liberal Democratic party. Japanese foreign policy may be characterized as one of "low posture." The keystone is the military alliance with the United States, under the terms of which America provides a "nuclear umbrella" and maintains air and naval bases on Japanese soil. Because of this protection, the Japanese have been in the fortunate position of having to spend less than 1 percent of their GNP for defense purposes, in contrast to the United States and the Soviet Union, which have been spending 10 to 15 percent, and England, France, and West Germany, which are in the 5 percent range. The low rate of expenditures for defense purposes has undoubtedly contributed to Japan's extraordinarily high economic growth rate (although this is obviously not the only factor).

Japanese leaders have consistently stated that they intend to continue the American alliance despite sharp criticism from the Left, which favors a neutralist policy. At the same time, there are increasing signs of a revival of nationalistic feelings, which for many years had remained rather quiescent. The trend is in the direction of a desire for a more independent foreign policy, and this coupled with the partial withdrawal from Asia on the part of the United States has had the effect of stimulating defense efforts in Japan. The Fourth Defense Build-up Plan beginning in the spring of 1972 has been announced. Under this plan, a little more than $16 billion (or about 0.92 percent of the GNP) is scheduled to be spent over a five-year period. This will represent the largest defense expenditure in Asia, excluding Communist China, and the seventh largest defense spending in the world. It would appear, however, that the stress still is on defensive rather than on offensive power. Japan has no strategic bombers, no battleships, no aircraft carriers, and no nuclear weapons. Although popular antipathy toward nuclear arms is clearly waning, it is highly improbable that Japan will seek to join the nuclear club, although the Japanese undoubtedly have the technical capability to build a nuclear arsenal. The situation could change, however, should there develop a proliferation of nuclear arms so that medium-sized nations like West Germany and India would go nuclear. Under those circumstances, Japan might be tempted for status reasons, if for nothing else.

Actually, there is little reason to believe, as Herman Kahn does, that economic and financial power will lead Japan to strive to become a military superpower. When a country has had a history of military expansion, it is perhaps natural that many people should fear the possible revival of militarism. But it is also worth remembering that the Japanese tried exercising military might some decades ago with results that were ultimately disastrous. Since 1945, the country has played a passive role both politically and militarily in international affairs, and the result has been economic prosperity. After all, military power will not necessarily get a nation more customers or ensure the sanctity of one's investments abroad, as recent American experiences seem to show. The Japanese people are a pragmatic people, and are likely to stay with a policy that has worked. Finally, the emergence of a Communist China armed with nuclear weapons has clearly changed the nature of politics in Asia. Where there was a vacuum before, there is now a commanding presence. No nation in Asia, including Japan, will want to challenge China in military terms. On the contrary, every nation in Asia, if not in the entire world, must, over the long haul, arrive at some sort of accommodation with this giant. It is a foregone conclusion that Japan will make every effort in this direction, and the fact that at least to date the Japanese have not felt a fear of China is an encouraging sign.

Further evidence of the Japanese effort to play down any potential military role in Asian affairs may be found in their foreign aid policy. The government has announced a policy of raising its foreign aid program to $4 billion a year by 1975, an amount approximately equal to 1 percent of the projected GNP. This would mean that the amount spent for aid to underdeveloped countries would be about equal to, or perhaps a little more than, the sums expended for defense purposes. This gives us some idea of the relative weights policy makers are giving to aid and to defense. So long as the world environment does not change drastically, it is hard to imagine that there will be marked shifts in these relative weights in the years ahead.

In short, in foreign relations, as in other matters, slow incremental change rather than drastic change is to be anticipated in the 1970s. The economy should continue to grow, although probably at a somewhat slower pace than was characteristic of the 1960s. The country should enjoy continued political stability, which will provide a favorable environment for the further maturing of democracy. Certainly the future will provide us with more empirical data for deepening our understanding of Japan's patron-client system of democracy, which may well become a prototype for democracy in other parts of the non-Western world.

Suggested Readings

1. Historical Background

Duus, Peter. *Feudalism in Japan.* New York: Knopf, 1969.

Maruyama, Masao. *Thought and Behavior in Modern Japan.* London and New York: Oxford University Press, expanded edition, 1969.

Reischauer, Edwin O. *Japan: The Story of a Nation.* New York: Knopf, 1970.

Sansom, George B. *The Western World and Japan.* New York: Knopf, 1950.

Smith, Thomas C. *The Agrarian Origins of Modern Japan.* Stanford, Calif.: Stanford University Press, 1959.

Ward, Robert E. (ed.). *Political Development in Modern Japan.* Princeton, N.J.: Princeton University Press, 1968.

2. The Economy

Ballon, Robert J. (ed.). *Doing Business in Japan.* Tokyo: Sophia University, 1967.

Broadbridge, Seymour. *Industrial Dualism in Japan: A Problem of Economic Growth and Structural Change.* Chicago: Aldine, 1966.

Guillain, Robert. *The Japanese Challenge: The Race to the Year 2000.* Philadelphia: Lippincott, 1970.

Kahn, Herman. *The Emerging Japanese Superstate: Challenge and Response.* Englewood Cliffs, N.J.: Prentice-Hall, 1970.

Lockwood, William W. (ed.). *The State and Economic Enterprise in Japan.* Princeton, N.J.: Princeton University Press, 1965.

Stone, Peter B. *Japan Surges Ahead: The Story of an Economic Miracle.* New York: Praeger, 1969.

Tsuneta Yano Memorial Society. *Nippon: A Charted Survey.* Tokyo (published annually).

Yamamura, Kozo. *Economic Policy in Postwar Japan: Growth versus Economic Democracy.* Berkeley and Los Angeles, Calif.: University of California Press, 1967.

3. The Individual, Group, and Society

Beardsley, Richard K., John W. Hall, and Robert E. Ward. *Village Japan.* Chicago: University of Chicago Press, 1959.

Dator, James A. *Soka Gakkai, Builders of the Third Civilization.* Seattle, Wash.: University of Washington Press, 1969.

Dore, R. P. (ed.). *Aspects of Social Change in Modern Japan.* Princeton, N.J.: Princeton University Press, 1967.

Ishida, Takeshi. *Japanese Society.* New York: Random House, 1971.

Nakane, Chie. *Japanese Society.* Berkeley and Los Angeles, Calif.: University of California Press, 1970.

Plath, David W. *The After Hours: Modern Japan and the Search for Enjoyment.* Berkeley and Los Angeles, Calif.: University of California Press, 1964.

Tsurumi, Kazuko. *Social Change and the Individual: Japan Before and After Defeat in World War II.* Princeton, N.J.: Princeton University Press, 1970.

Vogel, Ezra F. *Japan's New Middle Class.* Berkeley and Los Angeles, Calif.: University of California Press, 1967.

4. Political Institutions

Kubota, Akira. *Higher Civil Servants in Postwar Japan: Their Social Origins, Educational Backgrounds, and Career Patterns.* Princeton, N.J.: Princeton University Press, 1969.

Spaulding, Robert M., Jr. *Imperial Japan's Higher Civil Service Examinations.* Princeton, N.J.: Princeton University Press, 1967.

Steiner, Kurt. *Local Government in Japan.* Stanford, Calif.: Stanford University Press, 1965.

Von Mehren, Arthur T. (ed.). *Law in Japan: The Legal Order in a Changing Society.* Cambridge, Mass.: Harvard University Press, 1963.

5. Political Forces and Political Process

Cole, Robert E. *Japanese Blue Collar: The Changing Tradition.* Berkeley and Los Angeles, Calif.: University of California Press, 1971.

Dimock, Marshall E. *The Japanese Technocracy: Management and Government in Japan.* New York: Walker/Weatherhill, 1968.

Thayer, Nathaniel B. *How the Conservatives Rule Japan.* Princeton, N.J.: Princeton University Press, 1969.

Whitehill, Arthur M., and Shin-ichi Takezawa. *The Other Worker: A Comparative Study of Industrial Relations in the United States and Japan.* Honolulu: East-West Center Press, 1968.

Yanaga, Chitoshi. *Big Business in Japanese Politics.* New Haven, Conn.: Yale University Press, 1968.

6. Parties and Elections

Cole, Allan B., George O. Totten, and Cecil Uyehara. *Socialist Parties in Postwar Japan.* New Haven, Conn.: Yale University Press, 1966.

Fukui, Haruhiro. *Party in Power: The Japanese Liberal-Democrats and Policy-making.* Berkeley and Los Angeles, Calif.: University of California Press, 1970.

Scalapino, Robert A. *The Japanese Communist Movement, 1920–1966.* Berkeley and Los Angeles, Calif.: University of California Press, 1967.

_______ and Junnosuke Masumi. *Parties and Politics in Contemporary Japan.* Berkeley and Los Angeles, Calif.: University of California Press, 1962.

White, James W. *The Sokagakkai and Mass Society.* Stanford, Calif.: Stanford University Press, 1970.

7. Foreign Relations

Curtis, Gerald L. (ed.). *Japanese-American Relations in the 1970s.* The American Assembly. Washington, D.C.: Columbia Books, 1970.

Emmerson, John K. *Arms, Yen & Power: The Japanese Dilemma.* New York: Dunellen, 1971.

Hellman, Donald C. *Japanese Domestic Politics and Foreign Policy.* Berkeley and Los Angeles, Calif.: University of California Press, 1969.

Mendel, Douglas H. *The Japanese People and Foreign Policy.* Berkeley and Los Angeles, Calif.: University of California Press, 1961.

Weinstein, Martin E. *Japan's Postwar Defense Policy, 1947–1968.* New York: Columbia University Press, 1971.

index

A Note On The Type

The text of this book was set on the Linotype in Permanent, a distinguished new sans serif letter design. It was created by the European calligrapher Karlgeorg Hoefer to provide the designer with a letter that allows complete versatility in use and assures perfection in typographic quality. Designed with an exceptional blending of crisp lines, harmoniously related shapes, and a touch of contrast within the letter forms, Permanent combines an evenness of color in mass with superb clarity in detail to encourage maximum legibility and ease of reading. This new letter style has been adapted to linecasting matrices by Officine Simoncini of Bologna, Italy.

This book was composed by Cherry Hill Composition, Pennsauken, N.J., and printed and bound by Halliday Lithograph, West Hanover, Mass.